# Let's Hear a Story

# Let's Hear a Story

30 Stories and Poems for Today's Boys and Girls

SELECTED BY Sidonie Matsner Gruenberg

ILLUSTRATED BY DAGMAR WILSON

DOUBLEDAY & COMPANY, INC., GARDEN CITY, NEW YORK

## ACKNOWLEDGMENTS

The editor and publisher express grateful appreciation for the use of material listed below:

"The Big Day" by Blossom Budney. From THERE WAS ONCE A LITTLE BOY by Blossom Budney, © by Wonder Books, Inc., 1959. This story originally appeared in *Humpty Dumpty Magazine,* a subsidiary of the publishers of *Parents' Magazine,* under the title, "The Big Day."

BIG TALK by Miriam Schlein. Copyright 1955 by Miriam Schlein. Reprinted by permission of William R. Scott, Inc., publisher.

"Buildings" from WHISPERS *And Other Poems,* © 1958 by Myra Cohn Livingston. Reprinted by permission of Harcourt, Brace & World, Inc.

"Cheese, Peas and Chocolate Pudding" copyright © 1955, by the Bank Street College of Education. From the book BELIEVE AND MAKE-BELIEVE edited by Lucy Sprague Mitchell and Irma Simonton Black. Published 1956 by E. P. Dutton & Co., Inc. and reprinted with their permission.

CHOO CHOO by Virginia Lee Burton, copyright 1937 by Houghton Mifflin Company is reprinted by permission of and arrangements with Houghton Mifflin Company, the authorized publishers.

"Cooking" from WHISPERS *And Other Poems,* © 1958 by Myra Cohn Livingston. Reprinted by permission of Harcourt, Brace & World, Inc.

ELEPHANTS DON'T HAVE MANNERS by Leonore Klein. Copyright 1953 by Quality Magazine, Inc.

"E is the Escalator" from ALL AROUND THE TOWN by Phyllis McGinley. Copyright 1948 by Phyllis McGinley. Published by J. B. Lippincott Company. Reprinted by permission.

FLIPPY'S FLASHLIGHT by Corinna Marsh. Copyright, ©, 1959 by Corinna Marsh and Dorothy Teichman. Entire text reprinted by permission of E. P. Dutton & Co., Inc.

"Georgie Finds a Grandpa" reprinted from the Little Golden Book GEORGIE FINDS A GRANDPA by Miriam Young. Copyright 1954 by Simon and Schuster, Inc. and Artists and Writers Guild, Inc. By permission of Golden Press, Inc.

"Happy Birthday, Judy!" from HELLO, JUDY! by Charlotte Becker. Copyright 1941 by Charles Scribner's Sons. Reprinted by permission of the publisher.

"The Hatbox Cake" from OUR FRIEND MRS. GOOSE, by Miriam Clark Potter. Copyright 1951 by Miriam Clark Potter. Published by J. B. Lippincott Company and reprinted by permission.

JOHNNY LITTLEJOHN by Edith Thacher Hurd and Clement Hurd. Copyright © 1957 by Edith Thacher Hurd. Reprinted by permission of Lothrop, Lee & Shepard Co., Inc.

THE LITTLE FISHERMAN by Margaret Wise Brown. Copyright 1945 by Margaret Wise Brown. Reprinted by permission of William R. Scott, Inc., publisher.

LITTLE TOOT by Hardie Gramatky. Copyright 1939 by Hardie Gramatky. Reprinted by permission of G. P. Putnam's Sons, publishers.

"Moon-Come-Out" by Eleanor Farjeon from POEMS FOR CHILDREN, copyright 1933 by Eleanor Farjeon. Reprinted by permission of J. B. Lippincott Company and David Higham Associates, Ltd.

"A New Friend" by Marjorie Allen Anderson (June 1950 *Children's Activities*). Reprinted by permission of *Highlights for Children.*

THE "NOW-REALLY" TIME by Lilian Moore. Reprinted by permission of the author.

PIXIE, DIXIE, TRIXIE AND NIXIE by Dorothy and Marguerite Bryan. Copyright, 1938, by Rand, McNally, Inc. Reprinted by permission of the author.

THE RUNAWAY ROCKING HORSE by Lilian Robertson, copyright, 1948, by Harcourt, Brace & World, Inc. Reprinted by permission of the publisher.

SAMPSON, THE FIRE DOG by Alvin Tresselt. Copyright, Humpty Dumpty, Inc. Reprinted by permission.

"Singing-Time" by Rose Fyleman from THE FAIRY GREEN. Copyright 1923 by George H. Doran Co. Reprinted by permission of the publisher and The Society of Authors as the literary representative of the Estate of the late Rose Fyleman.

SPOODLES by Irma Simonton Black. Copyright 1948 by Irma Simonton Black. Reprinted by permission of the author.

"Surprise for Sally" reprinted from the Little Golden Book SURPRISE FOR SALLY by Ethel Crowninshield. Copyright 1950 by Simon and Schuster, Inc. and Artists and Writers Guild, Inc. By permission of Golden Press, Inc.

TEN LITTLE KITTENS by Elizabeth Coatsworth. Copyright, 1952, by Story Parade, Inc. Reprinted by permission of the author.

The editor is very grateful to her colleague Bella Koral whose wide knowledge in the field of stories for children has been an invaluable help in making this collection.

*For* MATTHEW ALAN,
*the youngest of our eleven grandchildren*

*Selected by Sidonie Matsner Gruenberg*

LET'S READ A STORY
LET'S READ MORE STORIES

# Introduction

DEAR MATTHEW:

I have selected these stories for you and for other boys and girls who like to hear stories as much as you do. I looked through many books trying to find the best stories that have to do with things you always want to hear about—lively boys and girls, birthday parties, kittens, puppies, kangaroos, horses and elephants, trains, tugboats, and grandpas. But I have also picked some stories about things which have not had so many stories and poems written about them like airplanes, tall buildings, flashlights, and escalators, and other things I never saw when I was your age. I hope you will have lots of fun having these stories read to you, looking at the pictures, and perhaps when you can, you will want to read them yourself.

SIDONIE MATSNER GRUENBERG

9

# Contents

11

# Let's Hear a Story

# Little Toot

*by Hardie Gramatky*

At the foot of an old, old wharf lives the cutest, silliest little tug-boat you ever saw—a *very* handsome tugboat with a brand-new candy-stick smokestack.

His name is Little Toot. And this name he came by through no fault of his own. Blow hard as he would, the only sound that came out of his whistle was a gay, small *toot-toot-toot.*

But what he couldn't create in sound, Little Toot made up for in smoke. From his chubby smokestack he would send up a volley of smoke balls which bubbled over his wake like balloons. Hence, when he got all "steamed up," Little Toot used to feel very important.

Then the flag at his masthead would dance like the tail of a puppy dog when he's happy.

And he flaunted his signals like a man-o'-war.

15

Now, the river where Little Toot lives is full of ships. They come from ports all over the world, bringing crews who speak strange tongues, and bringing even stranger cargoes—hides from Buenos Aires, copra from the South Seas, whale oil from the Antarctic, and fragrant teas from distant Asia. So there is always work for tugboats to do, either pushing ships into the docks to be unloaded, or else pulling them into the stream and down the channel to the ocean to begin a new voyage.

So a tugboat's life is a busy, exciting one, and Little Toot was properly right in the middle of it. His father, Big Toot, is the biggest and fastest tugboat on the river. Why, Big Toot can make *more* smoke and kick up *more* water than any two of the other boats put together.

As for Grandfather Toot, he is an old sea dog who breathes smoke—and tells of his mighty deeds on the river.

You'd think that Little Toot, belonging to such an important family, would have his mind on work. But no. Little Toot hated work. He saw no sense in pulling ships fifty times bigger than himself all the way down to the ocean. And he was scared of the wild seas that lay in wait outside the channel, beyond where the harbor empties into the ocean.

Little Toot had no desire to be tossed around. He preferred the calm water of the river itself, where he could always find plenty of fun. Like gliding, for example.

Or playing thread-the-needle around the piers.

Or, what was even fancier, cutting figure 8s.

Little Toot liked nothing better than to make a really fine figure 8. First you throw your weight on one side, then on the other. And the result never failed to delight him, although his antics annoyed the hard-working tugboats awfully.

But he kept on making figure 8s that grew bigger and bigger, until one day, carried away by the joy of it all, he made one so big it took up the whole river. Indeed, there was hardly room for it between the two shores, and no room at all for a big tug named J. G. McGillicuddy, which was bound downstream to pick up a string of coal barges from Hoboken. J. G. McGillicuddy had little love for other tugboats, anyway, and a frivolous one like Little Toot made him mad.

This by itself was bad enough; but, unfortunately for Little Toot, the other tugboats had seen what had happened. So they began to make fun of him, calling him a sissy who only knew how to play.

Poor Little Toot. He was ashamed and angry, but there was nothing he could do about it except blow those silly smoke balls.

But the more he blew, the more the other boats laughed at him.

Little Toot couldn't stand it. He fled to his favorite hiding place alongside the wharf, where his taunting friends could not reach him; and there he just sat and sulked.

After he had moped a while Little Toot saw, headed down the river, a great ocean liner.

And pulling it were four tugboats, with his own father Big Toot right up in front.

The sight of that brave, bustling work made Little Toot think. He thought harder than ever in his life, and then—all of a sudden—a great idea burst over him. He *wouldn't* be a silly, frivolous little tugboat any more. He would work like the best of them. After all, wasn't he the son of Big Toot, the mightiest tug on the river? Well, he would make Big Toot proud of him.

He'd show them all! Full of ambition, he eagerly started downstream.

He sidled hopefully up to one big ship after another, tooting for them to heave a towline. But they supposed he was still only a nuisance, and would have nothing to do with him. Oscar the Scandinavian rudely blew steam in his face, and the others were too busy with their own affairs to notice a bothersome little tug. They knew him too well!

But the rudest of all was a great transatlantic liner which blasted him right out of the water.

That was too much for Little Toot. He wasn't wanted anywhere or by anyone. With his spirits drooping, he let the tide carry him where it willed. He was so *lonesome*.

Floating aimlessly downstream, he grew sadder and sadder, until he was utterly miserable. He was sunk so deep in his own despair he didn't even notice that the sky had grown dark and that the wind was whipping up into a real storm.

But that wasn't all. Against the black sky climbed a brilliant, flaming rocket.

When Little Toot looked hard, he saw, jammed between two huge rocks, an ocean liner which his father had towed many times up and down the river.

Suddenly he heard a sound that was like no sound he had ever heard before——

It was the *ocean*—the great ocean that Little Toot had never seen. And the noise came from the waves as they dashed and pounded against the rocks.

It was truly a terrible thing to see.

Little Toot went wild with excitement! He began puffing those silly balls of smoke out of his smokestack.

And as he did, a wonderful thought struck him. Why, those smoke balls could probably be seen 'way up the river, where his father and grandfather were. So he puffed a signal.

'Way up the river they saw it.

Of course they had no idea who was making the signals, but they knew it meant "come quickly." So they all dropped what they were doing to race to the rescue.

Out from many wharves steamed a great fleet——
big boats, little boats,
fat ones, and skinny ones
with Big Toot himself right in the lead, like an admiral at the head of his fleet.

Just in time too, because Little Toot, still puffing out his S.O.S., was hard put to it to stay afloat.

One wave spun him around till he was dizzy; and another tossed him up so high that he was glad when a spiral-shaped wave came along for him to glide down on.

Before he could spit the salt water out of his smokestack, still another wave came along and tossed him up again.

It looked as though he'd never get down.

All this was pretty awful for a tugboat used to the smooth water of the river. What made it terrifying was the fact that, out of the corners of his eyes, when he was thus hung on a wave, Little Toot saw that the fleet wasn't able to make headway against such fierce seas.

Even Grandfather Toot was bellowing he had never seen such a storm.

Little Toot was scared green.

*Something* had to be done. But all that Little Toot had ever learned to do was blow out those silly smoke balls.

Where he was, the channel was like a narrow bottleneck with the whole ocean trying to pour in at once.

That was why the fleet couldn't make any headway. The force of the seas simply swept them back.

Indeed, they were on the verge of giving up entirely, when suddenly above the storm they heard a gay, familiar toot.

It was Little Toot—not wasting his strength butting the waves as they had done, but bouncing from crest to crest, like a rubber ball. The pounding hurt like everything, but Little Toot kept right on going.

And when Big Toot looked out to sea through his binoculars, he saw the crew on the great vessel throw a line to Little Toot.

It was a wonderful thing to see. When the line was made fast, Little Toot waited for a long moment——

And then, when a huge wave swept under the liner, lifting it clear of the rocks, he pulled with all his might. *The liner came free!*

The people on board began to cheer.

And the whole tugboat fleet insisted upon Little Toot's escorting the great boat back into the harbor.

Little Toot was a hero! And Grandfather Toot blasted the news all over the river.

Well, after that Little Toot became quite a different fellow. He even changed his tune.

And it is said that he can haul as big a load as his father can . . . that is, when Big Toot hasn't a very big load to haul.

# The Airplane

*(author unknown)*

*The airplane taxies down the field*
*And heads into the breeze,*
*It lifts its wheels above the ground,*
*It skims above the trees,*
*It rises high and higher*
*Away up toward the sun,*
*It's just a speck against the sky*
*        —And now it's gone!*

# When You Were Very Little

*by Betty Miles*

When you were very little
You lay in a basket.
You didn't run,
You didn't jump,
And you didn't say, "Hello."
You just lay in your basket, sleepy and dozy,
And sometimes you cried.

Then one day . . .

We looked in your basket.
You weren't sleeping,
And you weren't crying.
You were looking at us,

AND YOU WERE SMILING!

We were so pleased,
We said, "Look, you're smiling!
Our baby is smiling!"

When you were very little,
You rode in a carriage.
You didn't look out,
And you didn't wave.
You didn't watch dogs, you didn't see pigeons.
You just lay against pillows.

Then one day . . .

We looked in your carriage.
You weren't lying down,
And you surely weren't sleeping—

YOU WERE SITTING UP!

We said, "Look, you're sitting!
Now you'll watch people,
And dump-trucks, and birds!"

When you were very little,
You drank from a bottle.
You didn't have soup,
You didn't have plums,
And you didn't have ice cream.
You just drank from a bottle,
Lying and drinking.

Then one day . . .

28

We got out a spoon
And filled it with oatmeal.
You opened your mouth,
And leaned to the spoon.
There was some on your bib
And some on your fingers,
But some of it stayed on your tongue.

YOU WERE EATING!

When you were very little,
You didn't have teeth.
You had nothing to chew with.
We looked for a tooth when you opened your mouth,
But nothing was there.
Just a big empty smile.

Then one day . . .

You bit on your spoon,
And something went CLINK!
We looked in your mouth,

AND THERE WAS A TOOTH!

You were so pleased with your shiny new tooth,
You smiled and you laughed
To show us your tooth.

29

When you were very little,
You sat on the floor,
You sat in your playpen.
Wherever you were,
You just sat.

Then one day . . .

You started to move!
You leaned on your elbows
And pushed with your feet,

AND THEN YOU WERE CRAWLING!

We were surprised!
We said, "Look, you're crawling!"

When you were very little,
You said blub-blub-blub
And gling-gling-glung
And oidle-doidle-doidle.
You didn't say words,
You were too little.

Then one day . . .

We sat in the kitchen,
You lay in your bed,
And someone called, "Mom-my!"
We ran to your bedroom,
And heard YOU say, "Mom-my."

YOU WERE TALKING!

We were so proud,
We told everybody,

"OUR BABY CAN TALK!"

When you were very little,
You held onto a chair
And reached out to us.
You wanted to walk,
But you didn't know how.

Then one day . . .

We held out our arms.
We said, "Can you come over?"
You held out your hands,
You put down a foot,
Then the other foot, slowly.
Then the first one again, a little bit faster,
And you walked to our hug!

YOU COULD WALK!

AND LOOK AT YOU NOW!
  You can do everything!

You can climb to the top of the slide, and swoosh down!
You can sing, "Working on the Railroad"!
You can stir cake batter and lick the bowl!
You can make a sand pie in your pail!
You can take off your own shoes and socks!
You can roast marshmallows and eat them off the stick!
You can go to the toilet!
You can ride a bike!

   You can jump, jump, jump,

      And skip, skip, skip,

         And run, run, run,

Now that you're BIG
You can do EVERYTHING!

# Singing-Time

## by Rose Fyleman

*I wake in the morning early*
*And always, the very first thing,*
*I poke out my head and I sit up in bed*
*And I sing and I sing and I sing.*

# The Big Day

*by Blossom Budney*

There was once a little boy who wasn't *really* very little.

BUT——

His mother always said, "You are too little to leave the yard alone."

His father always said, "You are too little to go hunting with me."

His brother always said, "You are too little to run my electric train."

And his grandmother often said, when she came to visit, "Let's see what's in my bag for a fine little boy."

One day the little boy said, "I do not like being little. I will not be little any more!"

So he put on his cowboy boots and his father's old hat and he told his mother, "I am big now. I am going far away to visit Billy Adams today. Good-by."

His mother said, "Have a good time."

Off he went through a hole in the fence to visit Billy Adams next door.

34

When he came home all by himself, his mother said, "I'm glad you are big now. There is a big lamb chop for your lunch. And a big boy can help me set the table."

After lunch he told his mother, "I'm too big for a nap now. I think I'll just look at some books in my room." So he lay down on his bed to look at the books, because it's more comfortable that way, and guess what happened?

(Even big boys need naps sometimes.)

When he woke up again he went out with a piece of rope and an empty box. When he came back his dog was at the end of the rope, and there was a turtle in the box.

"I have been hunting," he told his mother. "Here are some of the wild animals I caught."

His mother could only say, "Gracious!"

She fed the wild one on the end of the rope. The wild one in the box she put in a shallow pan of water.

The boy took back his rope. He fastened it to a big long box. In the box he put a bear, a rabbit, a monkey who could dance, ten soldiers, and a fat clown.

They were all passengers.

Then he ran his train everywhere. Not just in one room on a track, but all over the world. In the house, on the porch, outside and back. He blew the whistle before each stop.

When the boy smelled dinner cooking he washed his hands all by himself.

When his father came home the boy told him all about how he went hunting.

When his brother came home the boy told him all about his round-the-world railroad.

And when his grandmother rang the doorbell he opened the door and said, "I have something for you." And he gave her a big kiss.

His grandmother was so surprised she just said, "Here is an Indian hat. I hope it's big enough for you."

At dinner the boy ate everything on his plate. Hunters get very hungry. And he drank a big glass of milk too.

Nobody said anything about bed. Big boys who have been all around the world on a train know when they're tired.

They remember about brushing their teeth, and usually they can button the buttons on their pajamas.

Then when his mother was ready to tuck him into bed the big boy said, "You may kiss me good night. I'm not too big for *that*."

So she did, and he went right off to sleep. He was very tired from the big day.

# Buildings

*by Myra Cohn Livingston*

*Buildings are a great surprise,*
*Every one's a different size.*

*Offices*
*grow*
*long*
*and*
*high,*
*tall*
*enough*
*to*
*touch*
*the*
*sky.*

*Houses seem*
*more like a box,*
*made of glue*
*and building blocks.*

*Every time you look, you see*
*Buildings shaped quite differently.*

# Happy Birthday, Judy!

*by Charlotte Becker*

It was Judy's birthday. She was four years old.
Judy washed and dressed in a hurry and ran downstairs.
"Happy birthday, Judy," said Mummy.
"Happy birthday, Judy," said Daddy.
"Woof," said Tippy. "Happy Birthday, Judy!"
Judy opened her presents.
The first one was a tea set.
Then a ball, and a monkey doll, and a doll carriage.
Oh, what a lovely birthday!
Judy played with her toys.
She played with them all morning.
But after lunch there was another surprise.
A BIG SURPRISE.

TO JUDY

The Express man left a big package on the porch.
"It's for you, Judy," Mummy said.
Judy called, "Peggy, Michael, come and see!"
Peggy and Michael lived next door.
They came running over.
"Happy Birthday, Judy!" they cried.
"I brought you a present," said Michael.
"I made it myself."
It was a boat.
"Thank you, Michael!" said Judy.
Then Judy's daddy helped them open the big box.
Guess what they found?
A little red table and four chairs.
"A tea party! A tea party!" said Judy.
"A tea party!" said Michael.
"Woof!" said Tippy. "Me too!"
So they set the table with the new tea set.
A cup and a plate for Judy.
A cup and a plate for Michael.
A cup and a plate for Peggy.
A cup and a plate for Tippy.
Then they all sat down.
"But we have nothing to eat," said Michael.
Just then the door opened.
Surprise! Surprise!
It was Judy's mother
with a beautiful birthday cake
and a pitcher of cocoa.
Puff-ff-ff!
Judy blew out the candles.

40

One, two, three, four! They all went out.
The children had cocoa and cake.
Tippy had some too.
Then they played "ring-around-a-rosy."
Ring-around-a-rosy
A pocketful of posy,
One, two, three,
All fall down!
The sun went down, down, down in the sky.
It was time for Michael and Peggy to go home.
"Thank you, Judy!" said Michael.
"We had fun at your party!"
GOOD-BY!

# Big Talk

*by Miriam Schlein*

A little kangaroo and a big kangaroo were holding a conversa-
tion.
"How high can you jump?" asked the big kangaroo.
"I can jump as high as the sun," said the little one.
"How fast can you run?" asked the big kangaroo.
"I can run as fast as the wind," said the little one.
"How much can you drink?"
"I can drink up the sea."
"How much can you eat?"
"All the grass in the world."
"Are you brave?"
"As a lion."
"Are you tall?"
"As a tree!"
"Have you a funny face?"
"Ah," said the little kangaroo.
"My face is as funny as a kookaburra and a koala bear dancing
in the moonlight!"
"Oh," said the big kangaroo.
"I'm glad you told me that.
Because, with all those other things you told me, I wasn't sure.
But now I know you're my own little kangaroo. Hop in."

The little kangaroo hopped into the pouch.

"But you will," said his mother.

The little kangaroo peeked up.

"Will what?"

"Will be brave as a lion, and grow tall as a tree, and jump high as the sun, and run fast as the wind."

"Will I really?" asked the little kangaroo.

"Oh, yes," said his mother, "I know."

"Ah," said the little one sleepily. "I'm glad you told me that. Because, you know, I really wasn't so sure about all those things myself!"

# Flippy's Flashlight

*by Corinna Marsh*

Once there was a little boy named Philip. But everybody called
him Flippy. Flippy had

    a BALL he could throw,

    a ROCKING HORSE he could rock,

    a furry toy KITTEN he could pat,

    big wooden BLOCKS

    he could build with,

    a CART he could pull,

    a TRAIN he could wind up,

    and a BOAT he could float in the bathtub.

But Flippy didn't know where any of them were. And he never
had time to look for them because Mommy always took him outdoors to play.

44

But one dark rainy day it rained so hard that Flippy couldn't go out. The park was all wet, and the streets were all wet, and the cars and buses were all wet, and the people were all wet too.

"Mommy, what can I do all day in the house?" Flippy asked.

"Well, let's see," said Mommy. "You can play with your TOYS. It seems to me you have enough TOYS for *ten* little boys."

"I guess I do," said Flippy. "I'll look for them."

So Flippy looked and looked for his BALL
and his furry KITTEN
and his wooden BLOCKS
and his CART
and his TRAIN that went *whirr-whizz-whirr* around the tracks, and the BOAT he could float in the bathtub.

But he couldn't find *any* of them!

Just then the doorbell rang.

"Hurry, Mommy! Let's see who it is," said Flippy.

Mommy opened the door. And there stood Flippy's grandma. Rain was dripping from her hat. Rain was dripping from her umbrella. And rain was dripping from the big shopping bag she held in her hand.

"What a wet, wet day!" said Grandma as she kissed Flippy and Flippy's mommy. Grandma took off her wet, wet galoshes, and Flippy put them in the bathroom. She hung her wet, wet raincoat on a hanger and let it drip, drip, drip into the bathtub. And she opened her wet, wet umbrella and put it on the kitchen floor to dry.

45

Flippy looked at Grandma's wet, wet shopping bag. Flippy waited. Almost always there was something in Grandma's shopping bag for him. What could it be this time?

"It's such a dark, rainy day," said Grandma, "I thought I'd bring Flippy a surprise that would make some dark places look light and bright."

And out of her shopping bag Grandma took a big FLASH-LIGHT.

"Oh, thank you," said Flippy. "But how does it work?"

"Like this," said Grandma, showing Flippy how to push the switch on the FLASHLIGHT. "Now you can see into all the dark places in your room—under the bed and behind the chair and everywhere."

"What fun," said Mommy. "I wonder what you'll find in all those dark places."

Flippy ran to his room. He flashed the FLASHLIGHT under his bed. And guess what he found!

There was a round ORANGE, of all things,

and a teeny, tiny, toy DUCK,

and a long PENCIL,

and a little square BOX,

and one of Flippy's MITTENS that had been lost ever since yesterday!

"Can you imagine that!" said Mommy. "Did *you* put all those things under the bed, Flippy?"

And Flippy said, "No, Mommy. I guess they just lost themselves there."

Then Flippy flashed the FLASHLIGHT behind the chair. And guess what he found!

There was his little tin DUMP TRUCK,

and a striped glass MARBLE,
and a rubber SPONGE,
and a RAG DOLL,
and one of Flippy's SOCKS that had been lost ever since yesterday!

"Can you imagine that!" said Mommy. "Did you put all those things behind the chair, Flippy?"

And Flippy said, "No, Mommy. I guess they just lost themselves there."

Then Flippy flashed the FLASHLIGHT into all the dark corners of the room. And guess what he found!
He found a PENNY in one corner,
and a WHISTLE in another corner,
and a COLORING BOOK in another
corner, and a little SILVER BELL.

48

And behind a pillow of the sofa he found a GOLD PIN that belonged to Mommy. And Mommy said, "Just imagine! I've been wondering where those things were. Did *you* hide all those things, Flippy?"

And Flippy said, "No, Mommy. They must have just lost themselves there."

Mommy laughed, and Grandma laughed too. "Things don't lose themselves, Flippy," said Grandma. "People lose them."

And Flippy said, "Then what people lost my BALL,
and my ROCKING HORSE,
and my furry KITTEN,
and my wooden BLOCKS,
and my CART,
and my TRAIN that goes *whirr-whizz-whirr* around the tracks,
and my BOAT that floats in the bathtub?"

"I wonder," said Mommy. And Grandma said, "Let's look. Maybe we can find them."

So Grandma and Flippy flashed the FLASHLIGHT into all the dark places they could find—behind things and under things and in the corners of the living room and in Mommy's and Daddy's bedroom and the dining room and the kitchen. But they couldn't find any of Flippy's lost toys anywhere.

But then Flippy and Grandma went back into Flippy's room. It was still raining hard outside, and the windows were all wet and gray and streaky with rain drops.

"Where *can* all those toys of yours be?" asked Grandma.

"I can't imagine," said Flippy flashing the FLASHLIGHT behind things and into all the dark places in his room.

"Do you suppose they could be in your toy box?" asked Grandma.

"Oh, no," said Flippy, "because if they were in my toy box, they wouldn't be lost. See?"

But when he opened the lid of the toy box and flashed the FLASHLIGHT into it, guess what he found!
There was his BALL,
and his ROCKING HORSE,
and his furry KITTEN,
and his wooden BLOCKS,
and his CART,
and his TRAIN that went *whirr-whizz-whirr* around the tracks,
and his BOAT he could float in the bathtub.

They weren't lost at all. They were just where Flippy had put them!

"You see," said Grandma, "your FLASHLIGHT can help you find lost things and things that *aren't* lost too."

"Just all the things you can't find," said Mommy with a smile.

And Flippy said, "It's just like magic!"

And so it was.

# Moon—Come—Out

*by Eleanor Farjeon*

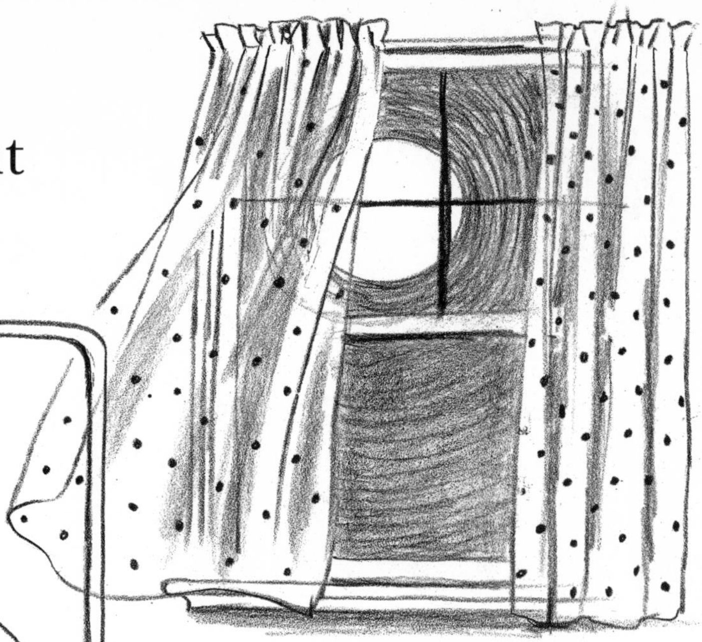

*Moon-come-out
And sun-go-in,
Here's a soft blanket
To cuddle your chin.*

*Moon-go-in
And sun-come-out,
Throw off the blanket
And bustle about.*

# The Hatbox Cake

*by Miriam Clark Potter*

The Animaltown people were having a Christmas fair in the schoolhouse. They were going to buy presents for each other there, and make money for the big Christmas party. They were getting it ready, one afternoon.

Mrs. Goose was making a soft fluffy cake with gooey white frosting for the refreshment booth. She had on her big blue-and-white-checked apron and her cooking cap. Her kitchen was full of delicious smells.

Mrs. Goose spread on the sweet, snowy frosting. She put it on thick! When the cake was all covered with it, she said, "There now, it's done. I'll take it over to the schoolhouse, quick. They'll be all ready to sell it."

"But what shall I put it in?" she asked herself. "The market basket is not wide enough. No, it won't fit in. Oh, what a pity! And I just can't carry it over on a plate."

She went into her bedroom and looked around. There was nothing on the bureau or the table to carry a cake in. Then she opened her closet door and looked up on the shelf.

53

Why, the very thing! She would use her hatbox. Her big green hat was in it, but she would take that out and put it on the bureau. Mrs. Goose hurried to the kitchen with the box. Yes, the cake fitted in nicely, without touching the sides at all. She was so pleased!

"Well, now I must clean up the kitchen," she told herself. What a mess! So many dishes to wash. Some flour spilled. Mrs. Goose washed and wiped and mopped and put things in order. She rinsed out the dishtowels and hung up the pan. Then she noticed the hatbox standing on the table.

"Why on earth did I bring my best hat into the kitchen," she wondered to herself, "when there were so many things in here already?" She took the box and plopped to the bedroom, rather in a huff. And she threw the box—yes, just threw it—up on the shelf. It went through the air and came down with a great big whack.

"Now," she said, "I must get ready to go to the school-house. I'll stay a while, and have a good time." She put on her blue dress and her red shoes, and then her best coat and hat. "I look nice," she said, as she passed her mirror. "Am I ready to go?"

But she felt she wasn't ready to go. "There is something else," she told herself. "Something I have forgotten. My purse? No, that is in my pocket. Oh, I know! The cake! Of course, the cake. That is what I was going to take with me to the school-house Christmas fair."

Mrs. Goose laughed happily and ran to the kitchen. But where was the cake? She looked all around. It was not on the shelf, or the table. Of course! It was in the market basket! But no; and then she remembered why she had not put it there. The

basket was not wide enough. She had put the cake into her hat-box, instead!

Then she remembered something else. She had thrown the hatbox up on the shelf with a terrific wham.

Oh, how awful! Mrs. Goose sat down on a chair. Well, she would take it anyway. Perhaps the cake was all right. But how could it be—when it was such a soft cake, and she had given it such a wham. She tried not to think about that.

Mrs. Goose took the box of cake and walked over to the schoolhouse. She opened the door to the big basement room where they were having the fair. There were little tables all around, and pretty things to sell on them. Aprons and napkins and warm socks and mittens, toys and blankets, and lots of other things. There was holly over the windows and a nice sign: "Welcome to the Animaltown Fair." Mrs. Goose's animal friends were all there, helping and buying. The refreshment booth was fitted up like a little restaurant. How busy and merry it all looked!

Mrs. Goose walked over to the refreshment booth, where her friends Mrs. Squirrel and Mrs. Pop-Rabbit were. "Here is my cake," she said.

"Oh good," said Mrs. Squirrel. "You were going to bring us one of your nice, soft chocolate ones, with gooey frosting."

"Yes," said Mrs. Goose. "It's very soft. And it's very gooey."

Mrs. Pop-Rabbit took off the cover, and she and Mrs. Squirrel looked into the box, smiling. Then their expressions changed. They did not smile; they looked horrified.

"Mrs. Goose," said Mrs. Pop-Rabbit, "did you drop this box on the way over? Your cake is just a mess of soft chocolate stuff, and bits of nuts and frosting, all swoozed together!"

Mrs. Goose craned her neck and took one look into the box. Then she began to cry. A tear slid off her bill.

"We can't sell it," said Mrs. Squirrel to Mrs. Pop-Rabbit.

Then Old Lady Owl looked at the cake. "Why, yes, we can," she said. "We'll take a scoop of the cake, frosting, nuts, and all—then put a scoop of white ice-cream on top—and call it Snowcap Chocolate Pudding. It will taste just delicious."

Mrs. Pop-Rabbit and Mrs. Squirrel looked pleased at that. So did Mrs. Goose. They did as Old Lady Owl had suggested. They even put a sign on the wall: "Try our delicious Snowcap Chocolate Pudding. Very unusual." The cake was scraped into a tin pail, and the hatbox was put under the table.

57

Then Black Cat came into the refreshment booth. "I'll try that pudding," he said. When he had eaten one dish of it, he asked for another.

In came Mrs. Hen and her chicken daughters. "We want some of that stuff that Black Cat is eating!" cried Arabelle and Clarabelle.

Other friends came. They all wanted some! Then Mrs. Goose saw that very soon the cake would be finished—the pail would be empty. She had a quick thought. She took the hatbox, rushed home, put on her blue-checked apron and her cooking cap, and made another cake just like the first one. Then she put it in the box and threw it up on the shelf again! "Now this cake will be just like the other one," she said, "all mashed and squashed and delicious."

She ran back to the fair, breathing hard. "Here is more cake for the Snowcap Chocolate Pudding," she said, and scraped it into the pail.

She was delighted! This cake went on selling just like the other. Then Mrs. Hen came up to the counter. "That pudding is so delicious," she said. "I should like to buy the recipe for it. Will you sell it to me? To make more money for the fair?"

"There's a surprise in it," Mrs. Goose said. "But I'll be glad to give it to you. I'll just skip home and copy it off."

Mrs. Goose found a piece of paper and a pencil and copied the recipes for the cake and frosting. Then she wrote at the end, "Now put the cake into a hatbox and throw it up on your closet shelf, as hard as you can. Then it will be in good condition to make Snowcap Chocolate Pudding, with ice cream on top." She wrote over the recipe, "Mrs. Goose's Hatbox Cake."

She rushed back to the fair. "Here it is," she said to Mrs.

Hen. "But don't read it over till you are ready to make it. Keep the surprise till then."

Mrs. Hen stared at Mrs. Goose as though she had said something very funny, but she paid for the recipe and put it in her pocket.

Arabelle and Clarabelle were giggling. "We want to know what the surprise is," they said. "Is it something special you do to the cake?"

"Yes," said Mrs. Goose, "it is something special you do to it, and you couldn't guess what!"

Then she laughed happily. Everyone was very merry at the fair. Things were selling; they were making money. The refreshment booth was a big success, for all the Animaltown people seemed hungry. The good smell of cocoa floated out on the air, and the Snowcap Chocolate Pudding went on and on. "I've heard of things selling like hotcakes," whispered Mrs. Squirrel to Mrs. Pop-Rabbit, "but never like mashed cakes!"

"It was Old Lady Owl's idea, really," said Mrs. Pop-Rabbit. "She is our wisest one."

Mrs. Goose was tired that evening, and was one of the first to go. After she went plopping out the door her friends were laughing and talking. "Well, for once she did a foolish thing that turned out to be fortunate," they said.

"Mrs. Goose's Hatbox Cake," laughed Mrs. Squirrel.

"Mrs. Goose's Hatbox Hit Cake," said Old Lady Owl. "Everyone liked it, when it was turned into pudding!"

"Thanks to you," they told her.

When Mrs. Goose got home she took off her best hat and looked up on the shelf for its box.

"Why, where did I put it?" she said.

Then she remembered that it was at the fair, under the table, all sticky.

"Never mind," she said. "I can keep my hat in the market basket."

Then she looked worried. "Tomorrow I must go back and get that box," she told herself. "I might want to make another cake."

# Spoodles

THE PUPPY WHO LEARNED

*by Irma Simonton Black*

Once there was a funny little dog. He wasn't quite a spaniel—
a spaniel looks like this.

He wasn't quite a poodle—

a poodle looks like this.

He looked like both of them at once, so he was called
Spoodles.

Of all the dogs in town—big dogs, little dogs, long dogs, short dogs, fat dogs, thin dogs—Spoodles was the only spoodle.

All the dogs liked Spoodles, but his best friend was Rowdy, who lived next door.

Spoodles was Connie's dog, and they played together a lot. The game they liked the best was chase-the-ball. Connie rolled the red ball and Spoodles raced after it and brought it back in his mouth.

Spoodles' family loved him very much.

Mother said, "What a good dog Spoodles is. He is better than a spaniel."

Father said, "He is better than a poodle."

Connie said, "He is as good as a spoodle, and that is very, very good."

But once Spoodles' family went away for the day. They couldn't take Spoodles with them, so they left him all alone in the house. Connie wasn't there to play ball with him. He couldn't get out to play with Rowdy.

Spoodles was LONELY! He put back his head and made his mouth in a round shape and

H   O   W   L   E   D   !

After he howled, he felt better, because he couldn't feel worse. If he couldn't play with Rowdy, he would have to find something else to do. He trotted sadly from one room to another. There was no one in the living room. There was no one in the dining room. There was no one in the kitchen. Sadly he climbed the stairs. Connie's room was empty. There was no one in the bathroom. But under Father's bed in the big front bedroom, Spoodles saw something hiding.

It was something furry hiding there under the bed, waiting

to pounce on him when he wasn't looking. Spoodles growled at it. Then he barked at it. Then he circled around it carefully, because it looked fierce. When he was behind it, suddenly he jumped on it, caught it by the throat, and shook it. It was quite a battle, but when it was over, Spoodles lay on the rug, dreamily chewing on Father's slipper.

After a while Spoodles began to get lonely again, so he went downstairs to look for something else to do. In the kitchen he found a tomato. It was round and red and roly, like a ball. Spoodles rolled it down the cellar stairs to see if it would bounce. It didn't. Spoodles needed another ball, so he went back to the vegetable bin. He took a second tomato carefully in his teeth and trotted upstairs with it. He went past Mother and Father's room, past the bathroom, straight into Connie's room, and he jumped up on Connie's bed.

He pushed the tomato with his nose and squeezed it between his teeth. That was the way he played with his ball. The tomato split open. He tried to play with it some more, but it was a very splashy ball, so he left it right in the middle of Connie's bed.

When he got back to the kitchen he smelled something good. The smell came from the garbage pail. First he found a piece of bread. That wasn't the good smell.

Then he found some orange skins.

That wasn't the good smell.

Then he found a pile of coffee grounds.

That wasn't the good smell.

He dug deeper in the garbage and out came some eggshells.

That wasn't the good smell.

At the very bottom Spoodles found a knobby soupbone.

*That* was the good smell!

When Spoodles had chewed the soupbone all he wanted, he looked for a place to bury it. The floor was too hard. He tried the sofa in the living room. That was better!

When the bone was buried, Spoodles felt sleepy, so he curled up and went to sleep. He wasn't lonesome any more.

A long time later, Spoodles woke up. He heard a tiny rattle. It was the sound of a key in the lock. His family were home! Spoodles ran to meet them, wagging his short tail so fast that it looked like several tails. Spoodles' family were glad to see him, too, until . . . Connie turned on the kitchen light.

"What a mess!" said Father as he started down the cellar stairs to look at the furnace.

Spoodles could tell by their voices that something was wrong. He wondered if *he* was wrong.

"Doggone that doggone slippery tomato! Nearly broke my doggone neck!" shouted Father as he got to the bottom of the stairs. Spoodles began to think for sure that he was wrong.

Even Connie didn't seem to understand about the ball game Spoodles had played with the tomato on her nice clean white bedspread.

"Look at this!" said Father, when he saw his slipper. "All chewed up. Insides pulled out. Heel gone."

By this time Spoodles was very, very sad. He wondered if his family would ever love him again.

But the worst of all was when they saw the living room.

Mother said, "He is worse than a spaniel."

Father said, "He is worse than a poodle."

Connie said, "He is as bad as a spoodle, and right now that is very, very bad."

"Where is Spoodles?" said Connie.

"Where is that bad little dog?" said Mother.

"Just wait till I get my hands on him" said Father, rubbing the bump on his head.

Suddenly Connie saw a small, sad black head peeping out from behind the big chair.

"Oh," she said. "Poor Spoodles! Look how sorry and worried he is!" Connie took Spoodles in her arms and hugged him tight. "Never mind, Spoodles," she said. "I still love you!"

"Well," said Connie's mother, "I don't love spilled garbage and slippery tomatoes and dirty bedspreads and chewed-up slippers and greasy, ripped-open sofas."

"Neither do I," said Connie's father, "but it was partly our fault too. We shouldn't have left so young a dog alone in the house all day. If we tell him never to do it again, I think he will understand."

"Spoodles, we won't ever leave you for so long," they said, "but you must never, never, never spill the garbage. You must never squash tomatoes on a bed. And never leave one on the cellar stairs. Or ever chew up slippers or bury another bone in the sofa. Not ever, ever, ever again."

Spoodles listened very carefully when they talked to him. He tilted his head to one side to hear better. Spoodles' eyes shone happily and the pink tip of his tongue hung out of his mouth. Then he kissed Connie right on the tip of her nose because she and her family still loved him.

# The "Now-Really" Time

*by Lilian Moore*

"Now really!"

That's what mothers were saying all over town.

"Now really, Susan, have you lost a mitten *again?*"

"Now really, Mary Jane, don't tell me you can't find your new blue gloves!"

"Now really, Michael Lee, where *is* your new red scarf?"

You could tell that the mothers were cross.

They said Susan instead of Susie, and Michael Lee instead of Mike.

68

The mothers were cross, but the children were having fun.

They lost so many things because they were out playing so much.

And they were out playing so much because of the snow.

Never had they seen such snow!

It kept coming down, down, down.

And never had the snow seemed so white or so soft.

Never had it seemed so right for snowballs and snowmen, for sleds and for forts.

Best of all, never had Big Hill been so much fun before.

Big Hill was right outside the town. Everybody said that Tommy Brown was lucky, because the hill started near his house.

It was always fun to play on Big Hill.

It was a hill that rose gently, right into the woods.

But now Big Hill was packed with snow, and all day long the children came to play there.

They walked up—puff, puff, puff.

They rode down on sleds. Look out below!

Oh, yes, there was lots of snow on Big Hill!

And the snow kept coming down!

But it was getting colder too—colder and colder. Noses were getting redder, and feet were getting so cold they hurt.

One day it was so cold that only two big boys were playing on Big Hill.

They had a snowball fight. One boy made a big fat snowball and threw it at his friend.

But he missed! The snowball sailed on and landed on the side of the hill.

And down the side of the hill it began to roll! It grew bigger and bigger. Then it rolled into a tree and stopped.

"Brr-rr-r!" said the boys. "It's cold!" And they ran home to get some hot cocoa and watch TV

Now it was very quiet on the snow-covered hill. A hungry squirrel came out of the woods. He was looking for nuts he had hidden. He pushed the snowball with his nose.

Away rolled the snowball.

Down, down the hill, getting bigger and bigger all the time.

Thump! It bumped into a tree again, and there it stayed.

That night a deer came out of the woods.

The deer stood by the tree, looking and listening. Then it turned and ran back into the woods.

But its leg kicked the snowball.

Down rolled the snowball, down the hill, getting bigger and bigger all the time.

Down, down, down.

Where would it stop?

Well, what a surprise *that* was!

When Tommy looked out his window next morning, he rubbed his eyes.

There in his backyard was a snowball. But what a snow-ball!

"Yippee!" yelled Tommy.

All his friends came to see the giant snowball that had rolled down from the hill.

Even grown-ups came to see it.

"It looks like something from outer space!" cried Mike.

"Let's play satellite!" cried Tommy.

So they put sticks here and there into the snowball and played it was Satellite X. When they got tired of that game, they played another.

"Let's make the Man from Mars," said Susie.

They took an old bike tire and cut it up.

They took an old mop.

They put a face and whiskers on the giant snowball. Then they played he was the Man from Mars.

For a whole week Tommy and his friends had fun with the snowball in Tommy's yard.

Then something happened.

The sun came out.

The days got warmer.

Warmer and warmer.

When you walked in the snow, it got mushy under your feet.

Little rivers ran from the snow into the streets.

And the snowball began to melt.

Slowly, slowly.

Drip by drip. Drip, drip, through the day. Drip, drip, all through the night.

One morning when Tommy got up and looked out his window, there was no snowball left at all!

He ran out into the yard to make sure.

No, there was no snowball.

But all over the yard there were many other things!

There was a red mitten.

There were blue gloves.

There was a red scarf.

There was even a brown rubber!

When the children came to play, they saw their things.

"Why, we lost them on Big Hill!" said Mike.

"And the snowball brought them down for us!" said Susie.

The mothers were surprised too.

But all they could say was, "Now really!"

# The Runaway Rocking Horse

*by Lilian Robertson*

Pinto was a rocking horse. He lived in a toyshop. Pinto had lived there all his life, but he wanted to see the world outside.

"No one ever looks at me," said Pinto sadly. "I'll never be sold. I wish I could be a policeman's horse or work on a merry-go-round. I wish I could be any other kind of horse but a rocking one. I could run away," thought Pinto. But how could he go anywhere on rockers?

Then SOMETHING happened. Pinto COULD move.

Happily he stepped off his rockers. Now he WOULD run away. Now he COULD be all the things he wanted to be.

"No more being a rocking horse for me!" said Pinto as he ran off.

All the toys waved good-by to him from the shop window.

Pinto galloped down the street, right through the village, as fast as he could go, straight to the blacksmith's shop.

"Now that I'm a real horse, I'll need real horseshoes," Pinto thought.

Pinto went into the blacksmith's, and when he came out, he had iron shoes under his hoofs that went "Clop-clop-clop-pity" when he ran.

"What a wonderful sort of noise!" said Pinto, and he ran around the blacksmith's yard just to hear the sound. He ran and ran until he couldn't run any more. Then he leaned on the fence to rest.

"Where are you going now?" asked a robin.

"To some nice place," Pinto answered.

"Then you mean a farm," said the robin.

"Everyone knows that's the nicest place of all."

Pinto ran off to see for himself.

76

The farm *was* nice. The animals were friendly and came to see him.

"May I stay here?" Pinto asked.

"Yes, if you work," the rooster told him. "Everyone works on a farm. The hay wagon would be too heavy for you, but you might be able to pull a plow."

Pinto ran off to try.

Pinto hitched himself to the plow. Then he tugged and pulled as hard as he could, but he couldn't move it.

"I think the plow is too big for me."

"And I think you are too small for the plow," laughed the Scarecrow. "Anyone can see you're not a plow horse at all. You have a saddle, and that means someone should ride you. A farm isn't the place for you."

Pinto ran away.

"I will get someone to ride me," Pinto said. "I'll join this fox hunt." But the dogs barked at him, and the horses laughed.

"You can't come with us," they said. "All you have is a little red saddle instead of a rider with a bright red coat. Everyone knows that a real saddle horse has to be trained to do exactly as he is told. You've never learned anything. You are a harness horse and the city is the place for you."

Then Pinto ran away.

"The city is the place to be," winked the lights to Pinto. "It's full of fun and excitement."

"And beautiful carriages too," added Pinto. "This is where I belong." He harnessed himself to a big carriage and ran up and down the city streets. But everyone who saw him laughed.

"Who ever heard of a pinto pulling such a fine carriage?" shouted a milk-wagon horse. "You should be pulling a pony cart."

Pinto left the carriage and ran away.

The pony cart wasn't nearly as elegant as the carriage. But Pinto didn't care. It was fun to be in the park all day. The children fed him sugar and popcorn and patted his nose.

"You must be a very special pony," they told him, "because you look so much like a cowboy's horse."

"A cowboy's horse, that's what I want to be," Pinto said. "Anyone can pull a pony cart. Nothing ever happens in the park. But out West there are stampedes and wild steers to chase. That's where I belong."

And Pinto ran away.

But it wasn't roundup time and the cattle just grazed and were lazy. They wouldn't even chase Pinto when he made faces at them. They just laughed and said, "You prance and dance and play the clown as if you belonged in a circus."

"A circus would be fun," said Pinto as he ran away.

Pinto ran right to the biggest circus in the land. It was exciting. He trotted along with the parade.

"I will be in one of the acts," Pinto said. But the circus animals laughed. "You have to know a lot of tricks to act in a circus. And you don't know any at all."

Pinto followed the circus from town to town. He hoped that someone would let him be in the show. But no one even noticed him.

Then one day the circus went to a little village. It was the one where Pinto's toyshop was.

"I wonder if the other toys missed me," Pinto thought. "And I wonder if my old rockers are still there." Then he ran away from the circus, straight to the toyshop. He kicked off the shoes the blacksmith had given him and went inside.

When the toys saw Pinto they cheered and crowded around him. Then they paraded through the shop.

"This is even better than a circus parade," said Pinto as he went to his rockers and climbed on them. "And my rockers feel better than the iron horseshoes."

"Everyone knows that a rocking horse belongs on rockers!" the toys all shouted at once.

Then all the toys hurried away to fetch brooms and brushes. They cleaned and polished Pinto until he looked like new.

"This is better than a farm or a fox hunt. It's better than

the city or the circus. It's the place where I belong," said Pinto.

But, best of all, someone wanted him.

When Pinto looked at the tag hanging from his new harness, he knew he'd never run away again.

# Cheese, Peas, and Chocolate Pudding

*by Betty Van Witsen*

There was once a little boy who ate cheese, peas, and chocolate pudding. Cheese, peas, and chocolate pudding. Cheese, peas, and chocolate pudding. Every day the same old things: cheese, peas, and chocolate pudding.

For breakfast he would have some cheese. Any kind. Cream cheese, American cheese, Swiss cheese, Dutch cheese, Italian cheese, blue cheese, green cheese, yellow cheese, brick cheese. Even Liederkranz. Just cheese for breakfast.

For lunch he ate peas. Green or yellow peas. Frozen peas, canned peas, dried peas, split peas, black-eyed peas. No potatoes, though—just peas for lunch.

And for supper he would have cheese and peas. And chocolate pudding. Cheese, peas, and chocolate pudding. Cheese, peas, and chocolate pudding. Every day the same old things: cheese, peas, and chocolate pudding.

Once his mother bought a lamb chop for him. She cooked it in a little frying pan on the stove, and she put some salt on it, and gave it to the little boy on a little blue dish. The boy looked at it. He smelled it. (It did smell delicious!) He even touched it. But . . .

"Is this cheese?" he asked.

"It's a lamb chop, darling," said his mother.

The boy shook his head. "Cheese!" he said. So his mother ate the lamb chop herself, and the boy had some cottage cheese.

One day his big brother was chewing a raw carrot. It sounded so good, the little boy reached his hand out for a bite.

"Sure!" said his brother. "Here!" The little boy *almost* put the carrot into his mouth, but at the last minute he remembered, and he said, "Is this peas?"

"No, fella, it's a carrot," said his brother.

"Peas," said the little boy firmly, handing the carrot back.

Once his daddy was eating a big dish of raspberry Jell-O. It looked so shiny red and cool, the little boy came over and held his mouth open.

"Want a taste?" asked his daddy. The little boy looked and looked at the Jell-O. He almost looked it off the dish. But: "Is it chocolate pudding?" he asked.

"No, son, it's Jell-O," said his daddy.

So the little boy frowned and backed away. "Chocolate pudding!" he said.

His grandma baked cookies for him. "Nope!" said the boy.

His grandpa bought him an ice-cream cone. The little boy just shook his head.

His aunt and uncle invited him for a fried-chicken dinner. Everybody ate fried chicken and fried chicken and more fried chicken. Except the little boy. And you know what he ate.

Cheese, peas, and chocolate pudding. Cheese, peas, and chocolate pudding. Every day the same old thing: cheese, peas, and chocolate pudding.

But one day—ah, one day a very funny thing happened. The little boy was playing puppy. He lay on the floor and growled and barked and rolled over. He crept to the table where his big brother was having lunch.

85

"Arf-arf!" he barked.

"Good doggie!" said his brother, patting his head. The little boy lay down on his back on the floor and barked again.

But at that minute, his big brother dropped a piece of *something* from his plate. And the little boy's mouth was just ready to say "Arf!" And what do you think happened?

*Something* dropped into the little boy's mouth. He sat up in surprise. Because *something* was on his tongue. And *something* was warm and juicy and delicious!

And it didn't taste like cheese. And it did *not* taste like peas. And it certainly wasn't chocolate pudding.

The little boy chewed slowly. Each chew tasted better than the last. He swallowed *something* and opened his mouth again. Wide. As wide as he could.

"Want some more?" asked his brother.

The little boy closed his mouth and thought. "That's not cheese," he said.

"No, it's not," said his brother.

"And it isn't peas."

"No, not peas," said his brother.

"And it couldn't be chocolate pudding."

"No, it certainly is not chocolate pudding," smiled his brother. "It's hamburger."

The little boy thought hard. "I like hamburger," he said.

So his big brother shared the rest of his hamburger with the little boy, and ever after that, guess what!

Ever after that, the little boy ate cheese, peas, and chocolate pudding and hamburger.

Until he was your age, of course. When he was your age, he ate everything.

# A New Friend

*by Marjorie Allen Anderson*

*They've taken in the furniture;*
*I watched carefully.*
*I wondered, "Will there be a child*
*Just right to play with me?"*

*So I peeked through the garden fence*
*(I couldn't wait to see).*
*I found the little boy next door*
*Was peeking back at me.*

# Choo Choo

THE STORY OF A LITTLE
ENGINE WHO RAN AWAY

*by Virginia Lee Burton*

Once upon a time there was a little engine. Her name was
CHOO CHOO. She was a beautiful little engine. All black and
shiny.

CHOO CHOO had a whistle which went who-WHOOOoo-
oo-oo! when she came to the crossing.

CHOO CHOO had a BELL which went DING! *DONG!* DING!
*DONG!* when she came to the station.

And a BRAKE which went s-ss-ss ssSSSSSWISH! And just
made an awful noise.

CHOO CHOO had an engineer. His name was JIM. Jim loved the little engine and took good care of her. He would shine and polish her till she looked like new and oil all the parts so they would run smoothly.

CHOO CHOO had a fireman. His name was OLEY. Oley fed the little engine with coal and water. The tender carried the coal and water.

ARCHIBALD was the conductor who rode in the coaches. He took the tickets from the passengers. Archibald had a big watch. He told the little engine when it was time to start.

CHOO CHOO pulled all the coaches full of people, the baggage car full of mail and baggage, and the tender, from the little station in the little town, to the big station in the big city and back again.

CHOO CHOO went through the fields and across the highway where the gates were down.

CHOO CHOO stopped at the little stations on the way to pick up passengers and baggage and mail to take to the big city. Ding-dong! Ding-dong! And she's off again. Through the tunnel and over the hills, down the hills, across the drawbridge, and into the big station in the big city.

One day CHOO CHOO said to herself, "I am tired of pulling all these heavy coaches. I could go much faster and easier by myself—then all the people would stop and look at me, just me, and they would say, 'What a smart little engine! What a fast little engine! What a beautiful little engine! Just watch her go by herself!' "

The next day CHOO CHOO was left alone on the tracks while Jim and Oley and Archibald were having a cup of coffee

in the restaurant. "Now is my chance!" said CHOO CHOO, and off she started. CHOO-choo-choo-choo-choo-choo! CHOO-choo-choo-choo-choo-choo! CHOO-choo-choo-choo! CHOO-choo-choo-choo! DING-dong! DING-dong! Who-WHOOOOOOO-OOOO! STOP, everyone! LOOK, everyone! STOP, LOOK, and LISTEN to ME! CHOO CHOO raced through the fields and she frightened all the cows and the horses and the chickens.

CHOO CHOO frightened all the people, and some clambered up the steeple. Choo-choo-CHOO-choo! Choo-choo-CHOO-choo! Choo-choo-CHOO-choo! CHOO-choo-CHOO!

CHOO CHOO whizzed by the crossings. All the automobiles and trucks had to put on their brakes so quickly that they piled one on top of another. My, they were mad at CHOO CHOO!

Over the hills went the little engine. Faster and faster. She couldn't stop now if she wanted to. The drawbridge was up!

CHOO CHOO jumped and just made it. But she lost the tender. Fortunately it fell on a coal barge which was passing under the drawbridge.

CHOO CHOO raced on, into the big yard in the big city. Swish! Swish! went the air brakes on the express trains. Poor CHOO CHOO didn't know which way to turn. Ah! There was a track out, a freight track that ran around the city. CHOO CHOO took it and escaped.

On and on went CHOO CHOO—out of the city through the suburbs, and into the country. It was getting dark! She had lost her way! She did not have much coal or water left, because she had lost her tender. Finally she came to where the tracks divided. One track went one way and the other track the other way. She did not know which track to take, so she took the track that went the other way.

It was an old, old track that hadn't been used for years. Bushes and weeds had grown between the ties. The trees had spread their branches over it. It was uphill and almost dark now—and this is how the poor, tired little engine went—— CHOOO-choo-choo-choo-ch-ch-CHOOoo . . . choo . . . choo-choooo . . . choo . . . ch . . . ch ch . . . ch . . . ch . . . ch-a-a-a-a-AH-*CHOO!* And there she sat!

In the meantime, when Jim and Oley and Archibald heard the little engine go by, they jumped up and ran after her. Jim called, "STOP! STOP!" But CHOO CHOO was too far away to hear even if she wanted to. Jim and Oley and Archibald ran and ran till they could run no more. Just then a Streamliner train came round the corner behind them. Jim took his red handkerchief and flagged it.

The Streamliner stopped.

Jim called to the Streamliner engineer, "Help me catch my runaway engine!"

"What about my schedule?" said the Streamliner engineer.

"Never mind your schedule," said Jim. "I must find CHOO CHOO." So he climbed in, and Oley and Archibald followed. Jim took the controls and—ZOOM!—they were off!

It was easy to see which way CHOO CHOO had gone. All the cows, horses, and chickens pointed with their tails or heads. The people at the crossing cried out, "She went that way, that way! Bring her back!" And the people in the town said, "Hurry! Hurry! Hurry and catch the little engine, the naughty, runaway engine before she does any more harm."

While waiting for the drawbridge to close, Oley cried out, "Look! There's the tender in that coal barge." Jim said, "Oley and Archibald, you stay here and get the tender up. I'll go on till I find CHOO CHOO."

Archibald telephoned for the train derrick. After it came it didn't take long to get the tender back on the tracks. They all went on to the "yard" by the big station to wait for Jim to come back with CHOO CHOO.

At last they came to the place where the tracks divided. They didn't know which way to go now. While they were deciding, an old man, who used to be an engineer when he was young, called out to them, "If you're looking for a runaway engine, she's right up that track there! And she won't be far, as it's an old track, which hasn't been used for well nigh forty years."

They turned on the big headlight and went slowly up the old track. They didn't go far before they saw the little engine. CHOO CHOO was so glad to be found that she blew one

"toot" with her whistle. There was just enough steam left for one small "toot." Jim took a big chain and ran to the little engine and hooked it on.

The Streamliner backed down the old track, pulling CHOO CHOO back to the main track, back through the big city, and back into the train yard, where Oley and Archibald were waiting.

They attached the tender and ran CHOO CHOO into the roundhouse and looked her over to see if any damage had been done. Except for being dusty and tired, she was as good as ever. Jim and Oley and Archibald were so glad to have CHOO CHOO back that they danced a jig together.

On the way home CHOO CHOO said to Jim, "I am not going to run away any more. It isn't much fun. I am going to pull all the coaches full of people and the baggage car from the little town to the big city and back again."

# Georgie Finds a Grandpa

*by Miriam Young*

When Georgie was six he started going to first grade. He learned how to read. He learned how to print. And he learned how to add. But he also learned that other children had something he didn't have.

Georgie had toys and books and an electric train. He had a tricycle and a kitten and a cocker spaniel. He even had a television set! But Georgie didn't have a grandpa. He didn't have any grandpa at all!

The boy who sat in front of Georgie had a grandpa who sent him oranges from Florida. The boy who sat beside him had a grandpa who could fix toys when they got broken.

And Georgie's best friend was always bringing picture books to school—his grandpa had a bookstore.

Georgie began to think of all the different kinds of nice grandpas there must be. If you could have a grandpa who worked in a bookstore, how about a grandpa who worked in a candy store!

Or a soda fountain!

Or a toy store!

Or suppose you had a grandpa who was a farmer and would let you drive the tractor!

Or who was a fireman and would let you ride the fire engine and ring the bell and pull the siren!

Or how about a grandpa who was an airplane pilot?

Or how about a grandpa who was a clown and could make you laugh all day?

One day a new boy came to Georgie's class. He had two grandpas! A faraway grandpa who sent him letters and things —and a nearby grandpa who read stories to him at night.

Georgie thought it very unfair that everybody had grandpas except him. He wanted a grandpa more than anything else in the world. "What could be more useful?" he thought. "What could be more fun?" Georgie decided to take matters into his own hands.

The next morning was Saturday. He took his wallet that still had his birthday dollar in it and walked down the road. At the corner there was an antique shop. Mrs. McMath, the owner, saw Georgie and waved.

"Hi there, where are you going so early?" she asked.

"On a trip," said Georgie. "I'm out hunting for something."

"Well, come here and get an apple to take along," said Mrs. McMath.

Georgie thought it would be a good idea to take an apple along in case he got hungry, so he went to the door of the shop.

"Georgie," said Mrs. McMath, as she gave him a nice red apple, "you've never been inside my shop. Wouldn't you like to see my antiques?"

"I don't know," said Georgie. "What are antiques, anyway?"

"Why, anything that is very old is an antique," she replied.

"In that case," said Georgie, "I'll come in and look around."

Georgie went into the shop. He saw a spinning wheel and a butter churn and a wooden cradle.

He saw a lot of old lamps and chairs. But he didn't want any of them.

Then, at the back of the shop, he saw an old man sitting in a rocking chair. He had white hair and white eyebrows and nice blue eyes. He smiled at Georgie.

And what do you think he was doing? He was making a tiny ship with a mast and two sails. And when the ship was finished, the old man folded it together and before Georgie could say, "Presto chango," the ship was inside a bottle, sails and all.

Georgie walked back to Mrs. McMath.

"Well," she said, "did you see anything you liked?"

"Yes," said Georgie, taking the dollar out of his wallet. "I'll take that." He pointed to the back of the shop.

"You mean you want that old rocking chair?" asked Mrs. McMath.

99

"I mean I want that old grandpa," said Georgie. "I'll take him home now."

"That's my father," said Mrs. McMath, "but you could have him after school and on Saturdays."

"Today is Saturday," said Georgie, and he walked back to the old man.

The old man was busy making another ship to fit inside a bottle.

"That's a nice ship," said Georgie. "How come you make such good ships?"

"Well," said the old man, "I used to be a sea captain. I used to sail all over the world."

"I'll bet you could tell a lot of good stories about ships and sailing," said Georgie.

The old man put down the ship and got up to stretch his back.

"The only trouble is," he said, "I haven't got anybody to tell stories to."

"You have now," said Georgie, taking his hand.

On Monday morning the boy who sat in front of Georgie brought an orange from his grandpa's orange grove. The boy who sat beside him brought in a car that his grandpa had fixed. And Georgie's best friend brought in some picture books from his grandpa's store.

But Georgie brought in something new.

"Where did you get such a beautiful ship?" asked the teacher. "And how did it get inside that bottle?"

"My grandpa did it," said Georgie. "My grandpa can do lots of things!"

101

# Timid Timothy

## THE KITTEN WHO LEARNED TO BE BRAVE

*by Gweneira Williams*

Once there was a little kitten named Timothy. He was black all over except for his four white paws and a little white bib under his chin. And he had two sets of black whiskers that stuck out fiercely from his face.

He looked like a big, brave, bold kitten. *But he wasn't.*

He was afraid of the rain on the roof. He was afraid of footsteps on the stairs. He was afraid of little mice. HE WAS AFRAID OF DOGS. So everyone called him 'Fraidycat. Everyone except his mother.

One day his mother said, "Timothy, you must learn to be a big, brave, bold kitten. We shall go to the zoo."

"Why?" asked Timothy, trembling.

"So I can teach you not to be afraid of other animals," said his mother, licking the fur the wrong way over his eye.

So they went to the zoo.

"Look at the lion," said his mother. "He won't hurt you. He's our cousin."

But Timothy shook with fright when the lion roared. "He's g-g-g-got big whiskers," he said. "B-b-bigger than mine!"

"Look at the bear," said his mother. "He's nice. He won't hurt you."

But Timothy shook with fright when the bear stood up on his hind legs. "He's g-g-g-got big claws," he said. "B-b-bigger than ·mine!"

"Look at the elephant," said his mother. "He's big but he's afraid of kittens."

But Timothy shook with fright when the elephant waved his trunk. "He's g-g-g-got a big nose," he said. "B-b-bigger than mine."

"Look at the rabbit," said his mother. "He's just a little bunny. He *can't* hurt you."

But Timothy shook with fright when the rabbit thumped his foot. "He's g-g-g-got big ears," he said. "B-b-bigger than mine!"

And Timothy ran all the way home.

His mother was very sad. "You must learn to be a big, brave, bold kitten," she said, blinking her big round eyes.

Timothy began to cry. "H-h-h-how?" he asked.

His mother said, "When you're afraid of anything, shoot out your whiskers. . . . Hump your back and make your fur stand up on end. . . . Wave your tail. . . . And say, loud as you can, 'P-s-s-s-s-s-s-s-s-s-s-t!' Like that. See?"

Timothy stood up. He shot out his whiskers. He humped his back and made his fur stand up on end. "P-s-s-s-s-s-s-s-s-s-s-s-t!" he said as loud as he could.

"That's fine," said his mother, licking the fur the wrong way over his eye. "Now go out and see how it works."

Timothy ran out of the house. He didn't meet a lion. He didn't meet a bear. He didn't meet an elephant. He didn't even see a rabbit.

But after a while he came to a toyshop.

"Perhaps," he said to himself, "I can find something to be afraid of in here."

He walked right in. The shop was full of toy animals. But Timothy thought they were real. So he shot out his whiskers and humped his back. He made his fur stand on end and began to wave his tail. Trembling all over, he went up to a stuffed lion and said in a whisper, "P-s-s-s-s-s-s-s-s-s-s-s-s-t!"

He expected the lion to roar. But the lion didn't say anything.

So Timothy, trembling just a little, went up to a toy teddy bear and said a little louder, "P-s-s-s-s-s-s-s-s-s-s-s-t!"

He expected the teddy bear to stand up on his hind legs. But the bear sat still.

So Timothy, hardly trembling at all, went up to a toy elephant and said much louder, "P-s-s-s-s-s-s-s-s-s-s-s-s-t!"

He expected the elephant to wave his big trunk. But the elephant sat still.

So Timothy, not scared one bit, walked up to a cotton flannel bunny rabbit with pink ears and said as loud as he could, "P-s-s-s-s-s-s-s-s-s-s-s-t!"

He expected the rabbit to thump his foot. But the rabbit sat still and didn't do anything.

So Timothy strutted out of the toyshop and started to go home.

"I'm a big, brave, bold kitten," he said to himself, "and I'm not afraid of anything, anything, ANYTHING! P-s-s-s-s-s-s-s-s-s-s-s-T!"

Just then he met a dog. A real live dog. It wasn't a big dog. It wasn't even a middle-sized dog. It was just a little baby dog. But Timothy was frightened just the same. He was so scared, he shook like a rattle.

Then he remembered what his mother had told him So he shot out his whiskers, humped his back, and made his fur stand right up on end. He waved his tail and said "P-s-s-s-s-s-t!" as loud as he could.

But he was so frightened he couldn't move.

The dog didn't run away. He walked right up to Timothy and sniffed at him. All over. His eyes got red. He began to growl. Timothy's whiskers almost fell off. Timothy shut his eyes tight and called for his mother, "M-i-a-a-a-a-a-a-a-a-o-w!"

The dog suddenly stood still. He looked scared to death. His eyes stopped being red. His tail went down between his legs. And then he turned and ran away as fast as he could.

Timothy was very surprised. "I scared a DOG!" he said.

He stuck out his chest. He waved his tail. And he strutted along home to tell his mother. He met her on the path by the next-door neighbor's garden.

"I'm a big, brave, bold kitten," he told her. "I scared a lion, and a bear, and an elephant, and a rabbit, and a DOG! I'm not afraid of ANYTHING!"

"That's fine," said his mother. "But . . ."

Then she stood still. Very still. They heard a humming noise. Like a top. Or maybe a small lion. It was very near. "B-z-z-z-z-z-z-z."

Timothy's mother picked him up by the scruff of his neck and ran home as fast as she could. When she put Timothy down, he was very angry. "Why did you run?" he asked in a big voice. "If it was a lion, I could have scared him. If it was a bear, I could have scared him. If it was an elephant, I could have scared him. Even if it was a dog, I could have scared him!"

"It wasn't a lion," said his mother. "It wasn't a bear. Nor an elephant. No indeed, or I would have let you scare them. It was BEES! THOUSANDS OF BEES!"

"Why didn't you let me scare them?" said Timothy.

"Because," said his mother, licking the fur the wrong way over his eye, "even if you are my big, brave, bold Timothy, you must learn not to go around LOOKING for trouble."

# The Little Fisherman

*A Fish Story Told by Margaret Wise Brown*

Once there was a great big fisherman and a little fisherman. They sailed boats. Only the big fisherman sailed a big boat and the little fisherman sailed a little boat. The big fisherman had big sailors on his boat—big sailors with big ropes and big buckets and big scrub brushes and big fish nets and big hammocks that they slept in at night. But the little fisherman had little sailors on his boat—little sailors with little ropes and little buckets and little scrub brushes and little fish nets and little hammocks that they slept in at night.

Very early in the morning just as the sun rose out of the sea, they went fishing. "Cast off!" shouted the big fisherman, and he pulled up his anchor and hoisted his sail. *"Cast off!"* shouted the little fisherman. And he pulled up his little anchor and hoisted his little sail. The wind blew up behind them and blew their boats away over the sea. They sailed over big waves and little waves. Big birds and little birds flew over them. Big porpoises and little flying fish and seal leaped out of the water into the air beside them. They sailed and sailed till the land behind them was out of sight and only the sea and the sky were all around them—the blue sea and the blue sky. Down below in the fishing grounds the fishes swam among the shadowy ledges of the sea.

The big fisherman heaved overboard a rope with a big piece of lead on the end of it to see how far the bottom of the ocean was.

THUD. The lead struck a rock on the bottom of the sea; the rope curled in the water.

"Not too deep and not too shallow. Here is where I will fish," said the big fisherman. "Lower away."

And his sailors lowered the big fish net into the sea.

Then up sailed the little fisherman and stopped his boat. He threw his little lead over and it sank deeper and deeper into the deep blue sea.

"Oh," said the little fisherman, *this is too deep for me.*" So he sailed a little farther and dropped his little lead. *"Click!"* The lead hit a rock on the bottom of the sea. The rope curled in the water. *"Here is where I will fish,"* said the little fisherman. *"Heave away!"* And his little sailors heaved his little fish net into the sea.

For seven days they fished for fish and they slept in their hammocks at night. They threw their nets over and they pulled the fish in. And they fished and they fished for the fish of the sea.

Hundreds of great big fish swam into the big fisherman's net.

Thousands of little fish swam into the little fisherman's net—thousands of little tiny, silvery shiny, wet and dripping, flipping flapping fish.

The big fisherman's boat was so full of fish that it sank low in the water. "Pull in the nets and head for home!" he shouted.

The little fisherman's boat was so full of fish that it sank low in the water. *"Pull in the nets and head for home!"* shouted the little fisherman.

The big fisherman sailed over big waves on a very big ocean. (There is no such thing as a little ocean. The ocean is always big.) And the wind blew behind them and filled their sails. And pretty soon they got there. Home.

And the people who wanted big fish bought the big fisherman's fish. And the people who wanted little fish bought the little fisherman's fish. And then the big fisherman put his hands in his pockets and went home. And the little fisherman put his hands in his pockets and went home.

The big fisherman went into his big house where his big family were waiting for him to have supper. And he took off his big boots.

And the little fisherman went into his little house where his little family were waiting for him to have supper. And he took off his little boots.

Then the big fisherman told his children a very little fish story.

And the little fisherman told his children A GREAT BIG FISH STORY.

# Pixie, Dixie, Trixie, and Nixie

THE STORY OF FOUR LITTLE PUPPIES WHO
GROW UP AND FIND HAPPY HOMES

*by Dorothy Bryan*

Four small cocker-spaniel puppies lived in a big box in a dog store.

Their names were Pixie, Dixie, Trixie, and Nixie.

Pixie was black.

Dixie was black too.

Trixie was white, with odd black patches that made him look very comical indeed.

Nixie was soft brown and the smallest puppy of all. His legs were too short and his ears were not as fine and long as those of his three handsome brothers.

Pixie, Dixie, Trixie, and Nixie were for sale, but no one came to buy a nice cocker-spaniel puppy for a long time.

So Pixie grew to be a strong, steady black dog.

And Dixie grew to be a very proud black dog.

And Trixie grew to be a funny, silly, spotted dog.

While little Nixie—well, little Nixie grew to be just a *nice* soft brown dog.

Now although Pixie, Dixie, Trixie, and Nixie were not unhappy living together in the dog store, still, each one did wish that someone would buy him and take him to a special home.

One day a kind-looking lady came into the store and spoke to the man there.

"I want a small, strong dog that would be good to a baby," she said.

The dog-store keeper led her over to where Pixie, Dixie, Trixie, and Nixie sat, all in a row. She looked them over carefully. She stopped a long time before Nixie, and Nixie looked longingly back at her. "This one looks *nice* enough for a baby, but he is really *too* small to take care of a baby. I will buy *this* one," she ended, patting Pixie on the head.

So then only Dixie, Trixie, and Nixie were left in the dog store, wishing for a home.

One day a proud-looking young lady came into the store and ordered, "I want a small, handsome dog that will ride with me in my automobile."

The dog-store keeper led her over to where Dixie, Trixie, and Nixie sat, three in a row. She looked them over briskly. When she turned toward Dixie, he put his nose high in the air and looked prouder than ever.

"I will buy *this* one," the young lady decided.

So then only Trixie and Nixie were left in the dog store, wishing for a home.

One day a jolly-looking man came into the store and called, "I want a small, lively dog that can act in my circus and make the children laugh."

The dog-store keeper led him over to where Trixie and Nixie sat, just two of them.

The jolly-looking man looked at Trixie and laughed. "Here is the silly circus dog I want to buy," he declared. He tweaked Nixie's ear, but it was Trixie that he tucked under his arm and carried away.

So then only little Nixie was left in the dog store, *wishing* for a home.

The dog-store man moved Nixie into a cage in the window, and there he sat all day, watching for someone to come along and want him.

One day Nixie saw Pixie trotting by, looking very important. And no wonder, for Pixie was taking care of, not one baby —but *two* babies in a carriage!

And little Nixie wished that *he* had somebody to take care of.

Another day Nixie saw Dixie go whizzing by, seated very proudly on the back of a shining automobile, with his ears flying out behind him.

And little Nixie wished hard that *he* had somebody to take *him* riding.

Another sunny day Nixie heard a loud burst of music, and a circus parade marched right by the window where he sat. There were brightly dressed ladies on prancing ponies and tumbling clowns riding in a donkey cart, and all sorts of animals—lions, tigers, a giraffe, monkeys in a gold cage, and, walking at the end of the circus parade, there was a line of big elephants. Last of all trudged a baby elephant, with Trixie riding gaily on his back, making all the children laugh.

And little Nixie wished *so* hard that *he* could ride in a circus parade.

Many days went by, and still little Nixie sat in the dog store, *wishing* for a home.

One morning a nice-looking lady came into the store with a little girl and said to the man, "I want to buy a dog for my little girl."

So the lady and the little girl started looking at all the dogs in the store—the big dogs and the small ones, the black dogs and the white ones and the brown ones too. Finally they came to Nixie.

"This is just little Nixie," the dog-store man said, starting to move by. But the little girl stood still.

"I like *him* best," she said.

"But he is not a very good cocker spaniel," the dog-store man argued. "His legs are too short, and his ears are too short too."

The little girl knelt down on the floor and took Nixie in her arms. "I don't care. He is the *nicest* dog. I like little Nixie better than any dog in the store—better than any dog in the world."

So Pixie, Dixie, Trixie, and Nixie each found the special home that he had wished for—but little Nixie was sure that his was the very *nicest* home of all.

# Johnny Littlejohn

*by Edith Thacher Hurd and Clement Hurd*

Once there was a boy, and
his name was Johnny Littlejohn.
He wanted to be a cowboy very much.

So his mother made him
a beautiful cowboy shirt.

Then she made him a pair
of furry cowboy chaps.

When Mr. Littlejohn came home that night, he brought a
real cowboy hat and a holster with two guns in it.

But Mr. and Mrs. Littlejohn said they were afraid that they could not buy boots for Johnny right now.

Johnny was sad that he could not have any cowboy boots, for he wanted them very much. But he put on all his other cowboy clothes and went out to be a cowboy. He saddled his pony and rode over the range. He roped little dogies and rounded up steers.

Then he galloped off to a rodeo.

But on his way to the rodeo, he met a Bad Guy, and the Bad Guy rode up to Johnny and said, "Reach for the sky, pardner, reach!" And Johnny reached.

Then the Bad Guy leaned over to take Johnny's guns, and Johnny said, "Oh, please, Mr. Bad Guy, don't take my guns, and I will give you my beautiful new shirt instead."

So the Bad Guy took Johnny Littlejohn's new shirt, and rode away, saying, "Now I'll be the handsomest bad guy at the rodeo."

Johnny Littlejohn rode on, and it was not long before
another Bad Guy came galloping over the prairie. And this Bad
Guy was quick on the draw as he shouted, "Reach!" Little
Johnny Littlejohn reached.

"Give me your guns," said the Bad Guy, but Johnny saw
that the Bad Guy had no chaps, so he said, "Look, Mr. Bad Guy,
don't take my guns, and I'll give you my new furry chaps
instead."

So the Bad Guy took Johnny Littlejohn's new furry chaps,
and rode away, saying, "Now I'll be the handsomest bad guy
at the rodeo."

Johnny Littlejohn rode on over the prairie, until all of a sudden a voice from the sagebrush shouted, "Reach, boy, reach!" And Johnny reached.

But when this Bad Guy came close to Johnny and told him to hand over his guns, Johnny said, "Why do you want my guns, Bad Guy? You already have two. If you won't take my guns, I'll give you my beautiful new cowboy hat instead."

"Ha-ha!" laughed the Bad Guy. "That's a funny one. Me? Wear your little hat?"

"It would keep your ears dry in the rain," said Johnny Littlejohn.

The Bad Guy thought for a moment and tried on the hat. He remembered how wet his ears always got in the rain, so he took Johnny Littlejohn's little new hat and went away, saying, "Now I'll be the handsomest bad guy at the rodeo."

Poor little Johnny Littlejohn rode on over the prairie without any shirt, without any chaps, and without any hat.

Just as he got near Rabbit Hole Ranch, where the rodeo was about to begin, he heard a terrible noise. It sounded like wildcats. It sounded like lions. It sounded like three men having an argument. Johnny Littlejohn jumped off his horse and crept behind a cactus.

There were all the Bad Guys sitting in a circle, talking, and shouting at each other.

"I am the handsomest bad guy at the rodeo!" shouted the first. "Look at my beautiful cowboy shirt."

"No, I am!" shouted the second. "See what fine chaps I am wearing."

"No, I am!" yelled the third. "I have a real cowboy hat to keep the rain out of my ears."

"No, I am!" "No, I am!" "No, I am!" They yelled all together.

At last they got so angry that they jumped up, took off their new clothes and hung them on a prickly-pear tree. Then they began to biff each other. Then they began to bop one another. They biffed and they bopped! They whammed and they slammed! They whopped and they popped! Round and round they went, whopping and popping, until they grabbed hold of each other's hair, and came wrangling and tangling right to the cactus where little Johnny Littlejohn was hiding.

But Johnny jumped behind his horse and watched as the Bad Guys ran round and round in a circle, shouting, "Ouch, ouch, let go my hair!" Johnny Littlejohn tried to stop them by calling, "Hey, you Bad Guys, stop fighting!"

But all the Bad Guys could answer was, "Ouch, let go my hair!" Then Johnny shouted even louder. "Hey, you Bad Guys, why have you taken off all your new clothes? Don't you want

123

them any more?" But all the Bad Guys could answer was, "Ouch, let go my hair!"

So Johnny Littlejohn crept out from behind his horse and over to the prickly-pear tree and put on all his new clothes again.

Then he stepped up to the Bad Guys and shouted: "REACH FOR THE SKY!"

The Bad Guys were so surprised that they stopped wrangling and tangling and put their hands over their heads.

Their eyes almost popped out when they saw who was talking.

"Now," said Johnny Littlejohn, "MARCH!" And Johnny Littlejohn marched the three Bad Guys off to the sheriff's.

The sheriff was very glad to get these Bad Guys, and he tied them to chairs with his lariat.

"There's a reward for these men," said the sheriff. And he handed Johnny Littlejohn three pieces of gold.

Johnny Littlejohn took the money and bought himself the most beautiful pair of cowboy boots in town.

And when he got home in his beautiful cowboy shirt and his beautiful cowboy chaps and his beautiful cowboy hat AND his beautiful new cowboy boots, Mr. and Mrs. Littlejohn could not believe their eyes.

"Where did you get those boots?" they asked.

Little Johnny Littlejohn just patted his trusty gun, but he wouldn't say . . .

NOTHIN'!

# Cooking

*by Myra Cohn Livingston*

*This will be a chocolate cake,*
*This a cherry pie,*
*This will be a doughnut*
*When the mud is dry.*

# Elephants Don't Have Manners

*by Leonore Klein*

There were once six elephants. They had never seen a horse. They had never seen a cow, a lion, or a monkey.

In fact, these six elephants had never seen anyone except five elephants.

*So*—when Lizzie got lost in the woods, they just stared and stared at her.

The oldest elephant stared at her curly blond hair. The youngest elephant watched the way she walked—on TWO FEET!

"What a funny nose she has," said the first elephant. "It's so very short."

"Can you pick up a peanut with your nose?" asked the second elephant.

Lizzie tried, but she couldn't. Her nose was too short.

"Let's water it, then," said the fifth elephant. "Flowers and grass grow when they are watered."

And all the elephants stood in a circle and showered Lizzie's nose with their long, curvy trunks. Lizzie's nose got all wet, but it didn't grow. Not an inch!

"What a pe-cu-liar little elephant," said all the elephants, flapping their ears with surprise.

"I'm not a pe-cu-liar little elephant," said Lizzie, stamping her foot. "I'm a little girl and I'm lost and I'm tired. If you'll carry me home on your backs," said Lizzie, "I'll show you what a little girl is and what she can do."

Lizzie climbed onto the sixth elephant's back, and the other elephants followed them out of the woods.

But all of a sudden the six elephants stopped.

"What's the matter?" asked Lizzie.

"It's the flies," said the first three elephants. "They tickle our backs."

"The flies?" said Lizzie. "Oh, I'll take care of them."

Lizzie climbed off the sixth elephant's back—up to the top of a palm tree she climbed. Down she came with a big palm leaf. And—SWAT! SWAT!—Lizzie swatted the flies on the six elephants' backs, until there weren't any flies left.

"Well," said the six elephants, all in one voice. "She can swat flies. She can climb trees. Thank you," said the six elephants. And off they went again.

But it wasn't very long before they stopped once more.

"What's the matter?" asked Lizzie.

"It's a fence," said the first three elephants. "We can't open a gate."

"A gate!" cried Lizzie. "Oh, I'll take care of that."

Lizzie climbed off the sixth elephant's back. She went to the gate, slipped up the hook, and pushed the gate open.

When the six elephants reached Lizzie's house, they stopped once more.

"What's the matter?" asked Lizzie.

"We're hungry," said the six elephants. "And we're thirsty too."

"Hungry!" cried Lizzie. "And thirsty too? Why, *do* come in and have some tea and cake."

Into Lizzie's living room walked the six elephants. It was a pretty tight squeeze.

Lizzie set the table. On it she put: SEVEN CUPS OF TEA, ONE SUGAR BOWL, ONE PLATE OF LEMON SLICES, ONE GOOEY CHOCOLATE CAKE, AND SEVEN NAPKINS.

"Help yourselves," said Lizzie.

The first elephant chewed up the napkins.

The second elephant sniffed up the sugar and sneezed and sneezed.

The third elephant popped a lemon slice into his mouth. It was sour, and he made a face.

The fourth elephant tried to balance a cup on his trunk. But the cup turned over and the hot tea spilled—all over his feet.

The fifth elephant put his foot into the middle of the chocolate cake. His foot got stuck and he couldn't pull it out.

The sixth elephant did nothing. He watched the other five elephants, and then he watched Lizzie.

"Come home," said the sixth elephant to the other five elephants. "Little girls aren't elephants and elephants aren't little girls, and they're both very different."

So Lizzie waved "Good-bye" to the six elephants, and the six elephants flapped their ears to Lizzie. And they all went home to the woods where they lived and had some nice green leaves and a cool drink from the water hole for their supper.

# Sampson, the Fire Dog

*by Alvin Tresselt*

In the firehouse around the corner from Billy's house lived a big
dog called Sampson. Sampson was mostly white, with black
spots all over him.

Poor old Sampson was such a lazy dog that all the firemen
called him Snoozy. He would spend the whole day sleeping in
front of the firehouse. But when the big brass bell clanged and
the firemen rode away on their shiny red fire truck, Sampson
would crawl into his bed under the stairs to sleep.

It was only when Billy came to play with him that Sampson really woke up. Then he would run and jump and bark. He and Billy were great friends.

One sleepy afternoon when the firemen were playing checkers and Sampson was sleeping, as usual, the big brass fire bell rang. Clang! Clang! The men stopped their checker game and grabbed their boots and rubber coats. "Come on, Snoozy," called the fire chief, "wake up and help us put out the fire!"

Sampson just looked at him sleepily and headed for his bed under the stairs.

"Don't bother with *him*," said the driver, "he's not worth his weight in soupbones."

Then, with a great roar, the shiny red truck with all the firemen hanging on sped down the street to fight the fire.

Sampson flopped down on his bed. Suddenly he sniffed—he smelled smoke!

He opened his left eye and he *saw* smoke! It was coming up from a pile of old rags right next to his bed!

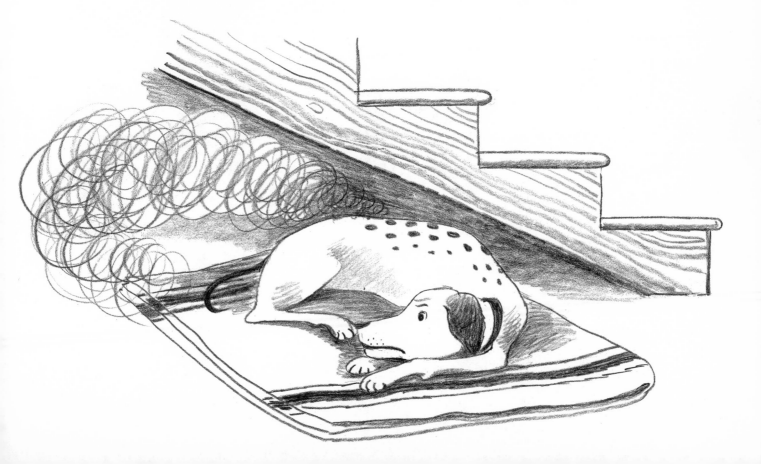

He scrambled to his feet and ran to the door, barking as loud as he could, but of course all the firemen were too far down the street to hear him.

He ran outside and barked, but there was nobody in sight. Just then he saw Billy coming home from school. He ran to him, barking. He tugged on Billy's sleeves, then ran back and forth to make Billy follow him. At first Billy thought it was a game. "Let me take my schoolbooks home first, Sampson," he laughed. "Then I'll play with you."

Just then he saw smoke beginning to come out of the firehouse door. Billy ran inside, grabbed a pail and quickly filled it with water, while Sampson led the way to the rags under the stairs. With a great *whoosh* of water Billy put out the fire. Then he carefully carried the smoky rags outside to be sure they wouldn't burn any more.

When the firemen finally rode back after putting out *their* fire, Billy and Sampson were sitting proudly in front of the firehouse with old fire hats on.

"Well, well," said the fire chief, "what's going on here?"

"We're firemen too," replied Billy. "The firehouse caught fire while you were away. Sampson discovered it, and *I* put it out! You can't call him Snoozy any more, he's wide awake now!"

Sampson just thumped his tail on the floor as loud as he could. With his fire hat over one eye he looked every inch a hero!

# Ten Little Kittens

*by Elizabeth Coatsworth*

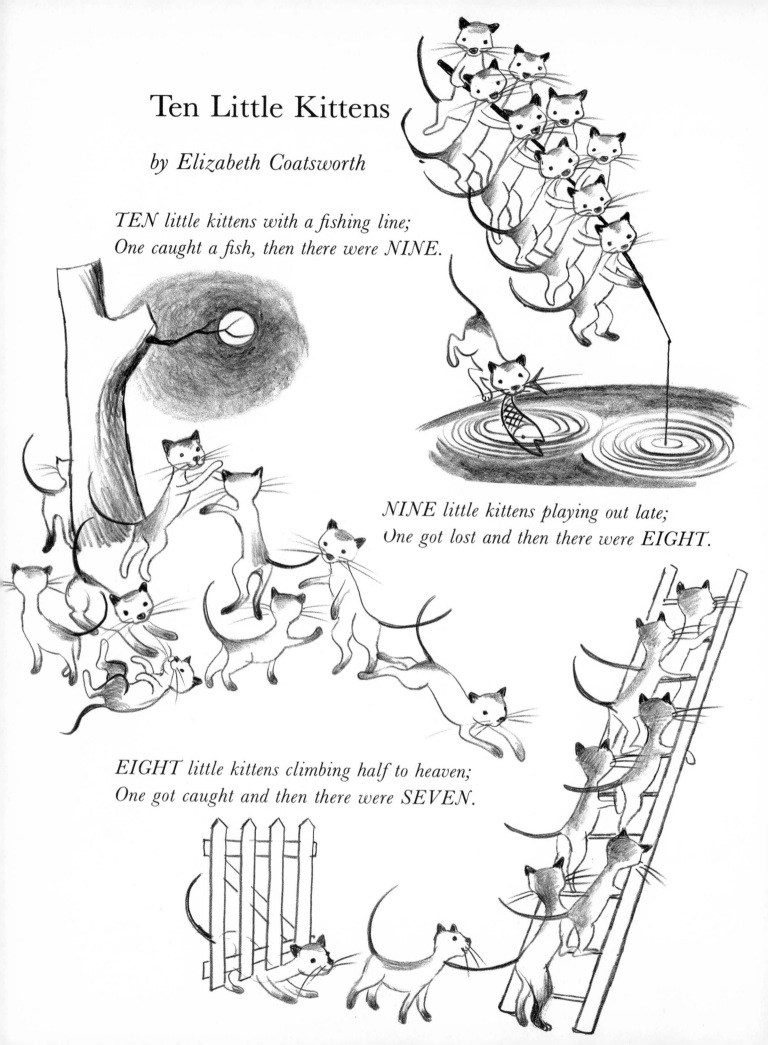

*TEN little kittens with a fishing line;*
*One caught a fish, then there were NINE.*

*NINE little kittens playing out late;*
*One got lost and then there were EIGHT.*

*EIGHT little kittens climbing half to heaven;*
*One got caught and then there were SEVEN.*

SEVEN little kittens, full of their tricks;
Daddy spanked one and then there were SIX.

SIX little kittens fooling round a hive;
Out came the bees and then there were FIVE.

FIVE little kittens going to the store;
One lost his penny and then there were FOUR.

FOUR little kittens sailing out to sea;
One fell overboard and then there were THREE.

THREE little kittens didn't know what to do;
One went to sleep and that left TWO.

TWO little kittens, with a great big gun;
Bang! it went off and that left ONE!

ONE little kitten sitting all alone;
Mummy called "Supper!" and then there was NONE.

# Surprise for Sally

*by Ethel Crowninshield*

Sally skipped down the street. She was very happy. It was her birthday, and she was five years old. She was singing a song as she skipped along the sidewalk, a song nobody knew but herself.

> *Hop, hop! Hop, hop!*
> *Hop over the crack.*
> *Hop, hop! Hop, hop!*
> *And never look back.*

She sang it over and over and never once touched a single crack in the sidewalk.

Sally's house was at the end of the street. Every day she went down to the stores to do errands for her mother.

Mother had said, "If you will promise not to cross the street, you may go to the store for me every day," and that is what Sally did. She promised, and she kept her promise, because that is what promises are for—to keep.

It was a long street and had lots of houses and stores.

139

There were apartment houses, and there was one house that stood all by itself in a garden with real flowers. Sally always stopped to look through the fence, and she made up a song for the flowers. The flowers always nodded to her. Sometimes she thought it might be the wind that made them nod, but then again she was sure they remembered her.

On, on down the street skipped Sally. There was the candy shop where she sometimes stopped if she had any pennies. There was the baker's, and then down almost at the end of the street was the shop she liked best of all.

It was the pet shop.

Every day, just before Sally came to it, she would stop skipping, put her hands over her eyes, and walk softly up to the window. She wanted the window to be a surprise, and it always was.

You could never tell what you would see. Sometimes there would be puppies climbing and falling over each other; sometimes goldfish, swimming in a big glass house; sometimes kittens; sometimes canaries singing in golden cages. Once there had been a parrot with red and green feathers. And once there had been a monkey.

Today, just before she came to the pet shop, Sally stopped skipping. She put her hands over her eyes and tiptoed up to the window. When she uncovered her eyes, she surely got a surprise. There was nothing in the window, nothing but one fat little black and white puppy dog with big, brown, frightened-looking eyes.

The puppy looked at Sally, and Sally looked at the puppy. Then she did something she had never done before. She went into the pet shop.

It was quite dark inside, and Sally couldn't see very well at first. There didn't seem to be anyone there at all, not even any pets.

"Good morning. Did you want something?"

It was the man who owned the pet shop, coming out of the back room.

"Where are all the pets?" asked Sally.

"Well, you see, I have to move," said the man, "and I have been selling everything. I have sold all but Snowshoes."

"Who is Snowshoes?" asked Sally.

"Why, that's Snowshoes in the window. She was the only puppy that wasn't sold."

"How much is Snowshoes?" asked Sally.

"Seeing she is the last pet I have, I'll sell her for five dollars," said the pet-shop man.

"Five dollars! I haven't that much money, except perhaps in my piggy bank at home."

The pet-shop man looked at Sally and began to smile. "I'll tell you what I'll do," he said. "You are the little girl who sings to the flowers in my garden every day. And you are the little girl who likes surprises. Now, if you will cover your eyes once more, I will give you a surprise."

Sally put both hands over her eyes.

"Now hold out your arms."

Something soft and warm tumbled into them.

"Oh, oh, oh! I will call you Sally Snowshoes because you belong to me!" Sally was laughing. So was the pet-shop man, and so was Snowshoes—Sally Snowshoes now.

"There's just one thing I want you to do," said the pet-shop man, "and that is to make up a song for Sally Snowshoes."

"I will. I will," laughed Sally. "Thank you! Thank you!"

Then Sally ran down the steps and home so fast that she did not care whether she stepped on the cracks in the sidewalk or not.

It was the best birthday she had ever had.

That night Sally remembered she had promised to make up a song for Sally Snowshoes, and because promises are made to be kept, she made up the nicest song she could.

# E Is the Escalator

*by Phyllis McGinley*

*E is the Escalator*
    *That gives an elegant ride.*
*You step on the stair*
*With an easy air*
    *And up and up you glide*
*It's nicer than scaling ladders*
    *Or scrambling 'round a hill,*
*For you climb and climb*
*But all the time*
    *You're really standing still.*

# Wiggles

*by Louise Woodcock*

One day Donnie went with his mother to see Mrs. Jones. Mrs. Jones lived on a farm. Donnie had never been there before.

Mrs. Jones said, "I'm so glad to see you, Donnie; go hunt around outdoors. You will find Wiggles to play with you."

Donnie didn't know who Wiggles was. A dog? A cat? A lamb? Or a mouse? He could have asked Mrs. Jones, but he didn't like to.

So he went out to look around.

The first thing he saw was a rabbit hutch. A big white rabbit was nibbling lettuce.

Could this rabbit be Wiggles? wondered Donnie.

Just then a big girl came from the barn. She was carrying eggs in a basket.

"Has this rabbit a name?" asked Donnie.

"We just call him Pinky," said the girl. "Because of his big pink ears." She went on into the house.

A squirrel whisked up a tree and sat on a branch over Donnie's head. He chattered and wiggled and twitched his tail.

Could he be Wiggles? wondered Donnie.

Just then a big boy came round the barn.

"Has that squirrel a name?" asked Donnie.

"Not that I know of," said the boy. "Most squirrels don't. Not wild ones, anyway." He went along to the pump.

Donnie walked past the barn. There in a pen were five little piglets with their mother. The piglets poked and nosed and wriggled their little curly tails.

Could all these little pigs be Wiggles? wondered Donnie.

There was an old man sitting near by on a chopping block.

"Have these little pigs got names?" asked Donnie.

"Not yet, son," the old man said, and went on sitting.

Donnie walked on along a lane and wondered and wondered.

Could Wiggles be these butterflies hovering over the clover?

Could Wiggles be these little chickens pecking, pecking?

Could this old mother hen be Wiggles?

Or the great rooster strutting around with his handsome tail?

How could you play with butterflies, or little chicks that ran so fast, or mother hens who squawked and fluttered away, or that big rooster looking proud and fierce?

Donnie walked on till he saw some cows in a field. A baby calf with wobbly legs was standing by its mother. There was a man there too, stroking the little calf's neck.

Could that calf be Wiggles? wondered Donnie.

"Has that little calf got a name?" he called to the man.

"My wife just calls him Pet!" the man shouted back. "Why don't you go find Wiggles? Down in the orchard."

147

Donnie wanted to ask him, "Who is Wiggles?"

He was afraid it might sound silly, so he walked toward the orchard.

There was a curly-haired dog just coming out of the orchard. He was sniffing the ground—sniff-sniff-sniff.

Could this be Wiggles? wondered Donnie. All the dogs he knew had names.

This one's might be Wiggles.

Then a little old woman hobbled out of the orchard. She was carrying apples in her apron.

Donnie asked her, "What is that dog's name, please?"

"Have an apple?" asked the little old woman, holding out her apron.

"Thank you," Donnie said and took one.

"His name's Jip," the old woman said. "Why don't you go find Wiggles? Last tree down this row. Come, Jip." She hobbled away. Jip trotted after her.

Donnie wondered what she could mean about the tree. Could Wiggles be a bird? How could you play with a bird?

He walked along the row of trees until he came to the last one. There was a ladder leaning against it.

"Hi," said a voice up among the branches. "Want to come up in my tree house?"

Donnie looked up and saw a boy looking down through the leaves.

"My name's Donnie. What's yours?" asked Donnie. He put one foot on the ladder.

"Wiggles," the boy replied. "Did you ever have a tree house?"

"No," said Donnie. He climbed another step. "But why do

they call you Wiggles?" he asked.

"Oh, just because I can wiggle my ears. Come up and I'll show you," Wiggles said.

So Donnie climbed up where he could see and Wiggles showed him.

# William and His Kitten

*by Marjorie Flack*

Once there was a little kitten, a little striped kitten, who was lost. It was lost on Pollywinkle Lane in the village of Pleasant-ville—lost on a Monday morning in May.

"Me-ew, me-ew, me-ew!" cried this little lost kitten, and it followed the people coming and going, up and down Polly-winkle Lane.

It followed the Milkman.
    It followed the Mailman.
        It followed the Grocery Boy.
But they paid no attention to the little lost kitty, because they were all much too busy.

It followed the fathers on their way to work.
    It followed the children on their way to school.
        It followed the mothers on their way to market.
But they paid no attention to the little lost kitten, because they were all much too busy.

Then it followed a small boy named William. The kitten followed William up and down and down and up the sidewalk of Pollywinkle Lane.

Now William was only four years old, so he was too young to be a Milkman. He was too young to be a Postman.

He was too young to be a Grocery Boy.
He was too young to be a father,
and he was too young to go
to the Pleasantville school.

So William was not too busy. He was not too busy to pay attention to the little lost kitten.

William stopped riding his scooter, and he patted the little kitten, and he said, "Nice little kitty, where did you come from?"

But all the little kitten could say was, "Me-ew, me-ew!"
So William did not know that this kitten was lost.

All morning long William played with the kitten.

At noontime William's brother Charles and his sister Nancy
came home from school.

"Hurry up, William!" they called. "Hurry up, William,
time for lunch!" And they ran into their white house on Pollywinkle Lane.

"I'm coming, I'm coming!" called William, and he ran into
the house after them. And then what did that little kitten do
but run right into the house after William, before he had time
to shut the door!

"My goodness me!" said their mother. "William, where-ever did you find that kitten?"

"But I didn't find him," said William, "he found me!"

"Me-ew, me-ew, me-ew!" cried the little kitten, and it sniffed the pleasant smell of food. "Me-ew, me-ew!"

Then William knew,
  and Nancy knew,
    and Charles knew,
      they all knew,
        that this little kitten was hungry,
          and it was hungry because it was lost!

"Poor little kitten," they all said together, and then they gave it some warm milk for lunch, and it lapped it all up until its tummy was as round as could be, and it no longer cried, "Me-ew, me-ew!" but sang, "Prrrrrr-prrrrrrr!"

"Please may I keep him?" William asked his mother. "I will call him Peter, and I will take good care of him, because he will belong to me."

"But it may have a name already," said his mother, "and it may belong to someone else."

"Oh, dear!" said William.

"Oh, dear!" said Nancy.

But Charles said, "What shall we do?"

"Now let me think," said their mother. "You might put a notice in the paper, or you might put a note in the post office, but the quickest way I know is to take it to the chief of police at the police station after school this afternoon. Tell him William found it, and if it has no home, we will give it one."

So after lunch William took good care of the little kitten

and he called it Peter all the time because he liked that name. When Nancy and Charles came back from school they helped William put the kitten in a market basket.

And down they all went, down Pollywinkle Lane, on their way to Main Street.

Then they passed by the drugstore. They passed by the grocery store. They passed by the church, and they passed by the post office, until at last they came to the police station.

There they met the chief of police, and he said, "How do you do, and what can I do for you today?" "William found a kitten, sir," said Charles.

"And it is here, sir," said Nancy.

And she held the basket, and William lifted the kitten out and put it on the desk.

"Well, well," said the chief of police, "well, well, I'll look in my book and see if anyone has lost a kitten."

So he looked in his book and he read:

*May 4*    *Lost: A striped kitten named Minnie. Phone Mrs. Finney at the post office. Reward.*

*May 6*    *Lost: A kitten with white paws named Mouser. Phone Mr. Smith at the grocery store. Reward.*

*May 8*    *Lost: A black and gray kitten named May. Call Mr. Poole at the Drugstore. Reward.*

"Well, well, well," said the chief of police. "There seem to be a lot of kittens lost lately."

Then he looked at the kitten and he saw that it had stripes, and he looked again and saw that it had white paws, and he looked again and saw that its colors were black and gray.

Then the chief of police said, "Well, well, well! I guess I had better telephone all these people. I can't tell if this kitten is one of the three lost kittens or not. If it is, William will get a reward."

So the chief of police telephoned Mrs. Finney at the post office, and Mr. Smith at the grocery store, and Mr. Poole at the drugstore, and they all said they would come right over.

First came Mrs. Finney, and she looked at the kitten and she said, "Yes, that is my little Minnie! My sister gave her to me last Monday, and Minnie stayed with me all Tuesday, but she ran away on Wednesday!"

Then along came Mr. Poole, and he said, "Yes, that kitten is May. She came to me on Saturday, but she ran away on Sunday."

157

Then in came Mr. Smith, and as soon as he saw the kitten he said, "Yes, it is Mouser. I found her at the store on Thursday, but she ran away on Friday!"

"Well, well," said the chief of police. "Mrs. Finney, you have found your kitten; Mr. Smith, you have found your kitten; and Mr. Poole, you have found your kitten. So that makes three rewards for William, and I can cross out all three notices in my book!"

"But they are all the same kitten!" said Mr. Smith.

"And it is only one kitten!" said Mrs. Finney.

"So whose kitten is it?" asked Mr. Poole.

And William said, "My mother said if it had no home, we would give it a home, sir."

"But this little kitten has three homes," said the chief of police.

Then Mrs. Finney said, "I wanted a cat to keep me company, but I will give Minnie to William for my reward."

And Mr. Smith said, "I wanted a cat to keep the mice away, but I will give Mouser to William for my reward."

And Mr. Poole said, "I wanted a cat to help me tend the drugstore, but I will give May to William for my reward."

"Well, well," said the chief of police. "Now William has three rewards, and I can cross out the notices in my book." And so he did, and he wrote "Found" after each one of them. Then he said to William, "Now you can take your kitten home with you, and watch out that it stays at home."

William said, "Thank you" to Mrs. Finney and to Mr. Smith and to Mr. Poole and to the kind chief of police.

Then Nancy and Charles and William took the little

kitten home to live with them in their white house on Pollywinkle Lane.

William always took very good care of his kitten, and it never ran away. He always called it Peter, although he knew its real name was Peter Minnie Mouser May.

Peter stayed at home with William a whole year.

Peter stayed with William all through the months of August through May, until another May came. And William was no longer four years old because he was five years old and going to school. And Peter was no longer a little kitten but a large, handsome cat.

Then early one morning in the month of May, when William called, "Here, Peter, here, Peter, come and get your breakfast!" no Peter came.

William called again, "Here, Peter, Peter, Peter, Peter, here, Peter, Peter!" and still no Peter came. Then William said,

"Oh, dear, oh, dear, Peter has run away!"

But just then William heard a strange little squeaking sound coming from Peter's basket near the stove in the kitchen.

He looked in the basket, and there William saw three tiny little kittens, three new little kittens, all cuddled up with their mother, and their mother was Peter! One of these kittens was striped, and so William named it Minnie. And one had white paws, so William named it Mouser. And the other one was black and gray, and so William named it May.

Peter took good care of her three little kittens, and they grew larger and stronger every day. And then one day when they were old enough to leave their mother, William put

Minnie
  and Mouser
    and May
      into the market basket.

Then William and Charles and Nancy took the basket full of kittens down Pollywinkle Lane and down to Main Street. First they stopped at the drugstore, and William gave Mr. Poole the black and white kitten named May, to help him tend the drugstore.

Then they stopped at the grocery store, and William gave Mr. Smith the kitten with the white paws named Mouser, to help keep the mice away.

Then they stopped at the post office, and William gave Mrs. Finney the striped kitten named Minnie, to keep her company. And——

Mr. Poole and Mr. Smith and Mrs. Finney were very pleased.